The Songs of Bilitis

Erotic Poetry in the Ancient Greek Form, Depicting Lesbianism and Illustrated in Neoclassical Art Deco Style

By Pierre Louÿs

Translated by Alvah C. Bessie

Illustrated by Willy Pogany

Published by Pantianos Classics

ISBN-13: 978-1-78987-241-5

First published in 1894

This reprint is based upon the English translation of 1926

Contents

iv

V

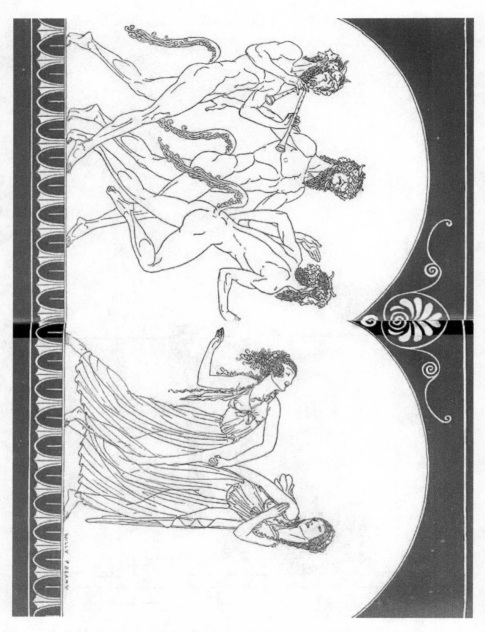

Exterior cover of the original 1926 Edition

The Translator's Dedication

... Τάδε νῦν ἑταίραις
ταῖς ἔμαισι τέρπνα κάλως ἀείσω.

- SAPPHO

The Author's Dedication

This little book of ancient love is respectfully dedicated to the young ladies of the society of the future.

The Life of Bilitis

Bilitis was born at the beginning of the sixth century before our era, in a mountain village situated on the banks of the Melas, towards the east of Pamphylia. This country is solemn and dreary, shadowed by heavy forests, dominated by the vast pile of the Taurus; streams of calciferous water spring from the rocks; great salt lakes remain on the highlands, and the valleys are heavy with silence.

She was the daughter of a Greek father and a Phoenician mother. She does not seem to have known her father, for he takes no part in the memories of her childhood. He may even have died before she was born. Otherwise it would be difficult to explain how she came to bear a Phoenician name, which her mother alone could have given her.

Upon this nearly desert land she lived a tranquil life with her mother and her sisters. Other young girls who were her friends lived not far away. On the wooded slopes of the Taurus, the shepherds pastured their flocks.

In the morning, at cock-crow, she arose, went to the stable, led out the beasts to water and busied herself with milking them. During the day, if it rained, she stayed in the *gynaeceum*, spinning her distaff of wool. Were the weather fair, she ran in the fields and played with her companions the many games of which she makes mention.

In respect to the Nymphs, Bilitis retained an ardent piety. The sacrifices she offered were almost always dedicate to their stream. She often spoke to them, but it seems quite certain that she never saw them, for she reports with so much veneration the memories of an old man who had one day surprised them.

The end of her pastoral life was saddened by a love-affair about which we know little, although she speaks of it at considerable length. When it became unhappy, she ceased singing it. Having become the mother of a child which she abandoned, Bilitis left Pamphylia for mysterious reasons, and never again saw the place where she was born.

=====

We find her next at Mytilene, whence she had come by way of the sea, skirting the lovely shores of Asia. She was scarcely sixteen years old, according to the conjectures of Herr Heim, who has established, with an appearance of truth, certain dates in the life of Bilitis from a verse which alludes to the death of Pittakos.

Lesbos was then the axis of the world. Halfway between lovely Attica and sumptuous Lydia, it had as capital a city more enlightened than Athens and more corrupt than Sardis: Mytilene, built upon a peninsula in sight of the shores of Asia. The blue sea surrounded the city. From the heights of the temples the white coastline of Atarnea, the port of Pergamum, could be seen.

The narrow and perpetually crowded streets shone with parti-colored stuffs, tunics of purple and hyacinth, cyclas [1] of transparent silks and bassaras [1b] trailing in the dust stirred up by yellow sandals. Great gold rings threaded with unfinished pearls hung from the women's ears, and their arms were adorned with massive silver bracelets, heavily cut in relief. Even the tresses of the men themselves were glossy and perfumed with precious oils. The ankles of the Greeks were bare amidst the jingling of their periscelis, [1c] great serpents of a light metal which tinkled about their heels; those of the Asiatics moved in boots of soft and painted leather. The passers-by stopped in groups before the shops which faced on to the streets, and where finery only was displayed for sale: rugs of sombre colors, saddle-cloths stitched with threads of gold, amber or ivory jewelry, according to the district. The bustle of Mytilene did not cease with the close of day: there was no hour, no matter how late, when one could not hear, through the open doors, the joyous sounds of instruments, the cries of women and the noise of dancing. Pittakos himself, who wanted somewhat to regulate this perpetual debauch, made a law forbidding flute-players who were too young to take part in any nightly revel; but this law, in common with all laws which attempt to change the course of natural customs, found no observance, but rather brought about a secret practice.

In a society in which the husbands were so occupied at night by wine and female dancers, it was inevitable that the wives would be brought together and find among themselves consolation in their solitude. Thus it came about that they were favorably disposed to those delicate love-affairs to which antiquity had already given their name, and which held, no matter what men may think of them, more of actual passion than of dissolute curiosity.

Then Sappho was still beautiful. Bilitis knew her, and speaks of her to us, under the name of Psappha, which she bore in Lesbos. No doubt it was this admirable woman who taught the little Pamphylian the art of singing in rhythmic cadences, and of preserving for posterity the memory of dearly cherished beings. Unhappily Bilitis gives few details about this figure today so poorly known, and there is reason for regretting it, so precious would have been the slightest word about the great Inspiratrix. In return she has left us, in thirty elegies, the story of her friendship for a young girl of her age named Mnasidika, who lived with her. We had already known this young girl's name, through a verse of Sappho's in which her beauty is exalted; but even this name was doubtful, and Bergk was nearly convinced that she called herself simply Mnaïs. The songs which will be read further on prove that this hypothesis should be abandoned. Mnasidika seems to have been a sweet and naïve young girl, one of those charming creatures whose mission it is to allow themselves to be adored; the more dear, the less effort they make to merit what is given them. Unmotivated loves last longest; this one lasted ten years. It will be seen how it was broken up through the fault of Bilitis, whose excessive jealousy could not understand the least eclecticism.

When she felt that there was nothing to keep her in Mytilene any longer except unhappy memories, Bilitis made a second voyage: she proceeded to Cyprus, an island both Greek and Phoenician like Pamphylia itself, and which must often have recalled to her the aspect of her native land.

It was there that Bilitis commenced her life for the third time, and in a fashion for which it will be more difficult for me to obtain sanction without again recalling how sacred a thing was love among the ancient races. The courtesans of Amathus were not fallen creatures, like our own, exiled from all worldly society; they were girls sprung from the best families of the town. Aphrodite had given them the gift of beauty, and they thanked the goddess by consecrating their grateful loveliness to the service of her cult. All cities which possessed, as did those of Cyprus, a temple rich in courtesans, cherished the same respectful solicitude over these women.

The incomparable story of Phryne, such as Athenaeus has handed it down to us, will give some idea of this kind of veneration. It is not true that Hyperides needed to display her nude in order to prevail upon the Areopagus, and nevertheless the crime was great: she had committed murder. [2] The orator removed no more than the upper part of her tunic and only revealed her breasts. And he begged the judges "not to put to death the priestess and the *Inspired of Aphrodite*." Contrary to the usage of other courtesans, who went about clothed in transparent mantles, through which all the details of their bodies were apparent, Phryne was in the habit of enveloping even her hair in one of those great wrinkled robes, whose grace has been preserved for us in the figurines of Tanagra. No man, if he were not one of her intimates, had ever seen her arms or shoulders; and she had never appeared in the pool of the public baths. But one day an extraordinary thing happened. It was the day of the Eleusinian festivals; twenty thousand people had come from all the countries of Greece and were assembled on the beach when Phryne advanced towards the waves: she took off her robe, she undid her girdle, she even removed her undergarment, "she unrolled all her hair and she stepped into the sea." And in this crowd there was Praxiteles, who designed the *Aphrodite of Cnidos* after this living goddess; and Apelles who caught a glimpse of his *Anadyomene*. Admirable race, to whom Beauty might appear nude without exciting laughter or false shame!

I would that this were the story of Bilitis, for, in translating her Songs, I fell in love with the little friend of Mnasidika. Doubtless her life was quite as marvellous. I only regret that it has not been further spoken of, and that the ancient authors, those at least who have survived, are so poor in information about her. Philodemus, who pilfered from her twice, does not even mention her name. In default of happy anecdotes, I beg that all will be good enough to be content with the details that she herself gives us about her life as a courtesan. That she was a courtesan cannot be denied; and even her last songs prove that, if she had the virtues of her vocation, she also had its worst weaknesses. But I am concerned only with her virtues. She was pious and devout. She remained faithful to the temple as long as Aphrodite consented to prolong the youth of her purest worshipper. The day she ceased being loved she ceased to write, she says. However, it is difficult to suppose that the songs of Pamphylia were written during the time they were being lived. How could a little mountain shepherdess have learned to scan her verses according to the difficult rhythm of the Aeolic tradition? It would be found more plausible that, grown old, Bilitis pleased herself in singing for herself the memories of her far-off childhood. We know nothing about this last period of her life. We do not even know at what age she died.

Her tomb was rediscovered by Herr G. Heim, at Paleo-Limisso, by the side of an ancient road not far from Amathus. These ruins have almost disappeared in the past thirty years, and the stones of the house in which Bilitis may have lived pave the quays of Port-Said today. But the tomb was underground, according to the Phoenician custom, and it had even escaped the depredations of treasure-hunters.

Herr Heim penetrated into it through a narrow well filled with earth, at the bottom of which he found a walled-up door which it was necessary to demolish. The low and spacious cavern, paved with slabs of limestone, had four walls, covered with plaques of black amphibolite, upon which were carved in primitive capitals all the songs which will be read hereafter, with the exception of the three epitaphs which decorated the sarcophagus.

There it was that the friend of Mnasidika rested, in a great terra-cotta coffin, beneath a lid modeled by a careful sculptor who had carved in the clay the face of the dead: the hair was painted black, the eyes half-closed and lengthened by a pencil, as in life, and the cheek scarcely softened by a slight smile born from the lines of the mouth. No one will ever solve the mystery of these lips: both clear-cut and pouting, both soft and dainty, touching each on each, but still as though drunk to kiss and clasp again. [3]

When the tomb was opened she appeared in the state in which a pious hand had laid her out twenty-four centuries before. Vials of perfume hung from earthen pegs, and one of them, after so long a time, was still fragrant. The polished silver mirror in which Bilitis saw herself, the little stylus which spread blue paint upon her eyelids, were found in place. A little nude Astarte, relic forever precious, still watched over the skeleton, decked with all its golden jewels and white as a branch of snow, but so soft and fragile that the moment it was breathed upon it fell to dust.

PIERRE LOUŸS
Constantinople, August 1894.

[1] *cyclas*: a rich robe of circular cut, worn by women;

[1b] *bassaras*: a mantle or cloak;

[1c] *periscelis*: anklets.

[2] *she had committed murder*: This is not strictly accurate. Phryne was accused of profaning the Eleusinian mysteries, at that time a crime infinitely greater than any possible assassination. It is likely that Louÿs took the liberty of changing this detail in order to bring the "enormity" of the crime into a modem focus.

[3] *No one will ever*: The French has it, "Rien ne dira jamais ce qu'étaient ces lèvres…" This is one of those phrases which, although pregnant with subtle implications in the original, successfully defies all attempts at accurate translation.

I - Bucolics in Pamphylia

Ἀδὺ δέ μοι τὸ μέλισμα, καὶ ἤν σύριγγι μελίσδω
κἤν αὐλῷ λαλέω, κἤν δώνακι, κἤν πλαγιαυλίῳ
THEOCRITUS

[1]

THE TREE

I undressed to climb a tree; my naked thighs embraced the smooth and humid bark; my sandals climbed upon the branches.

High up, but still beneath the leaves and shaded from the heat, I straddled a wide-spread fork and swung my feet into the void.

It had rained. Drops of water fell and flowed upon my skin. My hands were soiled with moss and my heels were reddened by the crushed blossoms.

I felt the lovely tree living when the wind passed through it; so I locked my legs tighter, and crushed my open lips to the hairy nape of a bough.

PASTORAL SONG

One must sing a pastoral song to invoke Pan, God of the summer wind. I watch my flock, and Selenis watches hers, in the round shade of a shuddering olive-tree.

Selenis is lying on the meadow. She rises and runs, or hunts grasshoppers, picks flowers and grasses, or bathes her face in the brooklet's cooling stream.

I pluck the wool from the bright backs of my sheep to supply my distaff, and I spin. The hours are slow. An eagle sails the sky.

The shadow moves; let us move the basket of flowers and the crock of milk. One must sing a pastoral song to invoke Pan, god of the summer wind.

MATERNAL COUNSEL

My mother bathes me in the dark, she dresses me in the sunlight and coifs me in the soft glow of the lamp; but if I go out in the moonlight she ties my girdle and makes a double knot.

She tells me: "Play with the virgins, dance with the little children; do not look out of the window; fly the conversation of young men and fear the widow's counsel.

"Some evening, someone, as has always been, will come to lead you over the threshold in the midst of a great cortège of sounding drums and amorous flutes.

"That evening, when you go out, Bilitis, you will leave me three gourds of gall: one for the morning, one for the afternoon, and the third, the bitterest, for the festival days."

BARE FEET

I have long black hair down my back, and a little round cap. My frock is of white wool. My sturdy legs are browning in the sun.

If I lived in town I should have golden trinkets and gold-embroidered frocks and silver slippers... I look at my naked feet in their slippers of dust.

Psophis! come here, little creature! carry me to the brook, bathe my feet in your hands, and press some olives with some violets, to scent them among the flowers.

Today you shall be my slave; you shall follow me and serve me, and at the end of the day I will give you some lentils from my own garden ... to give your mother.

THE OLD MAN AND THE NYMPHS

An old blind man lives on the mountain. For having looked at the nymphs his eyes have long been dead. And from that time his happiness has been a far-off memory.

"Yes, I saw them," he told me: "Helopsychria, Limnanthis; they were standing near the bank, in the green pool of Physos. The water shimmered higher than their knees.

"Their necks were bent beneath their heavy hair. Their nails were filmy, like the wings of grasshoppers. Their breasts were deep, like the calyx of the hyacinth.

21

"They trailed their fingers upon the water, and pulled long-stemmed lilies from the unseen silt. About their separated thighs, slow circles spread..."

SONG

Torti-tortue, what are you doing there? --I am winding wool and I spin Milesian thread. --Alas! alas! Why don't you come and dance? --I am so sad. I am so sad.

Torti-tortue, what are you doing there? --I cut a reed to make a funeral pipe. --Alas! alas! And tell me what has happened. --I'll never tell. Oh, I shall never tell.

Torti-tortue, what are you doing there? --I am crushing olives to make a funeral oil. --Alas! alas! And who has died, mayhap? --How can you ask? Oh, say, how can you ask?

Torti-tortue, what are you doing there? --He fell into the sea... --Alas! alas! and tell me how was that? --From his white horses' backs. From his white horses' backs. [2]

PEDESTRIAN

One evening, as I sat before my door, a young man passed me by. He looked at me, I turned away. He spoke to me, I did not answer him.

He would have come nearer. I took a scythe that leaned against the wall and should have split his cheek had he advanced one pace.

Then, stepping back a little, he began to smile, and blew across his hand, saying: "A kiss for you." I screamed and wept. My mother ran to me,

Anxiously, thinking I had been stung by a scorpion. I cried, "He kissed me." My mother kissed me too, and bore me off in her arms.

AWAKENING

It is already daylight. I should have long arisen. But morning sleep is sweet, and the warmth of the bed keeps me snuggled up. I want to stay still longer.

Soon I'll go to the stable. I'll give grass and flowers to the goats, and a skin of fresh water, drawn from the well; and I shall drink out of it just as they.

Then I'll tie them to the post and draw the milk from their warm udders; and, if the kids are not jealous, we all shall suck the soft teats together.

Did not Amalthea [3] give suck to Zeus? Then I shall go. But not yet. The sun arose too soon, and mother has not yet awakened.

RAIN

Softly and in silence the fine rain has moistened everything. It is still raining a little. I am going to stroll under the trees. Bare-footed, not to soil my sandals.

The spring rains are delicious. Branches laden with rain-soaked blossoms daze me with their perfume. The delicate skin of the bark shines in the sun.

Alas! how many blooms have fallen to earth. Pity the fallen flowers. Pray do not sweep them up, or crush them in the mud: but leave them to the bees.

Beetles and snails promenade in the pathways between the pools of water; I do not wish to tread upon them, nor frighten this gilded lizard which stretches and blinks its eyes.

FLOWERS

Nymphs of the woods and fountains, beneficent friends, oh! here I am. Do not hide yourselves, but come to my aid, for I am sorely overburdened by the weight of so many plucked flowers.

I shall choose from among you a poor hamadryad with lifted arms, and into her leafy hair I'll thrust my heaviest rose.

See! I have taken so many from the fields that I shall never be able to carry them home, unless you make me up a huge bouquet. If you refuse, take care:

Yesterday I saw the nymph whose hair is tinted orange served like a beast by the satyr Lamprosathes, and I shall denounce the shameless creature.

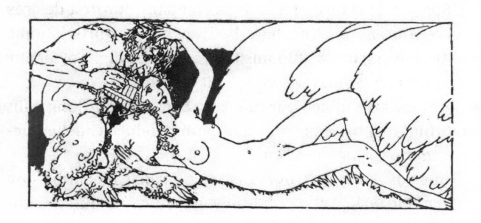

IMPATIENCE

I threw myself weeping into her arms, and for long minutes she felt my warm tears flowing over her shoulder before my anguish allowed me once again to speak:

"Alas! I am only a child; the young men will not look at me. When shall I have lovely young breasts like yours, to swell my gown and tempt their kisses?

"No one glances with avid eyes when my tunic slips; no one picks up the flower that falls from out my hair; no one tells me that he'll kill me if my lips should know another's."

Tenderly she answered me: "Bilitis, little maid, you cry like a cat in the moonlight and are worried without reason. The most impatient virgins are not those the soonest chosen."

COMPARISONS

Sparrow, [4] bird of Kypris, accompany our first desires with your notes. The new body of young girls blooms with flowers, just as blooms the earth. The night of all our dreams arrives and we whisper it together.

At times we match our different beauties, our long hair, our budding breasts, our quail-plump deltas, couched beneath the springing down.

But yesterday I strove this way against Melantho, my elder. She was proud of her bosom, which sprouted within the month, and, mocking at my flattened tunic, called me Little Child.

No man could possibly have seen us, we showed ourselves nude before the other girls, and, if she won upon one point, I vanquished her by far upon the others. Sparrow, bird of the Kyprian, accompany our first desires with your notes.

THE STREAM IN THE WOOD

I bathed alone in the stream in the wood. I must have frightened the poor naïads, for I could scarcely see them far away in the dark water.

I called to them. To mimic them I plaited iris blossoms, black as my hair, about my neck, twined with knots of yellow gilly-flowers.

With a long floating weed, I made myself a green girdle, and to see it I pressed my breasts and inclined my head a little.

And I called: "Naïads! naïads! play with me, be nice." But the naïads are transparent, and perhaps I even caressed their lissom arms, unknowing!

PHITTA MELIAI

As soon as the sun's heat diminishes, we will go and play on the banks of the river; we will struggle for a frail crocus, or for a sopping hyacinth.

We will make a human necklace, and we'll weave a wreath of girls. We will take each other by the hand, and grasp each other's tunic-skirts.

Phitta Meliai! give us honey! Phitta Naïades! let us bathe with you. Phitta Meliades! shade sweetly our perspiring bodies.

And we will offer you, oh! beneficent nymphs, no shameful wine, but oil and milk and many crook-horned goats.

THE SYMBOLIC RING

Travelers coming from Sardis speak of the necklaces and precious stones with which the Lydian women deck themselves, from the tops of their tresses to their tinted feet.

The young girls of my country have neither bracelets nor diadems, but their fingers bear a silver ring, upon the scroll of which the triangle of the goddess is engraved.

When they turn the apex outward, it signifies; "Psyche to be taken." And, when they turn it inward: "Psyche taken."

The men believe in it, the women don't. As for myself, I scarcely notice the direction of the apex, for Psyche is an easy catch. She is always to be taken.

MOONLIGHT DANCES

Upon the soft grass, in the night, young girls with violet hair have danced together, and one of each pair gave the lover's answer.

The virgins said: "We are not for you." And, as though they were ashamed, they shielded their virginity. An aegipan played a flute beneath the trees.

The others said: "But you will come to seek us." They fashioned their dresses after the manly garb, and languidly struggled and twined their dancing limbs.

Then, each declaring herself to be subdued, she took her comrade by the ears, cup-fashion, and, tilting her head, she drank a lengthy kiss.

LITTLE CHILDREN

The brook is nearly dry, the drying rushes perish in the mud; the air is burning, and far from the steep embankments a thin clear streamlet flows upon the sand.

There it is from morn to night that little naked children come to play. They bathe, no higher than their calves, so sunken is the stream.

But they tramp in the current and often slip upon the rocks, and little boys throw water upon little laughing girls.

And when a company of passing merchants leads down their great white cattle to the sink, they cross their hands behind them, and watch the heavy beasts.

STORIES

I am beloved by little children; when they see me come they run to me and tug upon my tunic, and grasp my legs about with tiny arms.

If they have gathered flowers, all are mine; if they have caught a beetle, they place it in my hand; if they have nothing, they fondle me and make me sit before them.

Then they kiss me on the cheek, they rest their little heads upon my breasts; they supplicate me with their shining eyes. How well I know just what they mean to say!

They mean: "Bilitis sweet, tell us again, for we are good, the story of the hero Perseus, or else how little Helle met her death." [5]

HER FRIEND, MARRIED

Our mothers carried us together, and tonight Melissa, my dearest friend, was married. The roses still are lying on the road; the torches still are flaming, flaming...

And I return by the same path with mother, and I dream. Thus, what she is today, I also might have been. Have I grown up so soon?

The cortege and the flutes, the marriage song; the flowered carriage of the bridegroom, all these pomps some other night will spread themselves about me, among the olive branches.

Just as Melissa now, I shall disrobe myself before a man and taste of love by night, and later still small babes will feed upon my swollen breasts.

CONFIDENCES

The next day I went to visit her, and we blushed the moment that we saw each other. She had me come into her private room, that we might be alone.

I had many things to tell her; but when I saw her I forgot them all. I did not even dare to throw myself upon her neck, I looked at her high girdle.

I was astonished that her face remained the same, she still seemed to be my friend; and yet, since the night before, she had learned so many things that maddened me.

Suddenly I sat upon her knees, I took her in my arms and whispered wildly in her ear, most anxiously. She put her cheek to mine and told me all.

THE MOON WITH BLUE EYES

At night the hair of women and the willow's branches merge and mingle softly with each other. I walked upon the water's edge. Suddenly I heard a singing voice: 'twas then I knew there were some maidens there.

I said to them: "What do you sing?" They answered me: "We sing of those returning." One waited for her father, one her brother; but she who waited for her lover was the most uneasy.

They had plaited crowns and garlands for themselves, cut palms from the palm-trees and dragged the lotos from the pond. They had their arms about each other's necks, and sang alternately.

I wandered on along the river's edge, sadly and alone, but, looking all about me, I perceived the blue-eyed moon had risen behind the trees, to see me home.

SONG

Shades of the wood where she now ought to be, tell me, whence has my fair mistress strayed? --She has gone down to the plain. --Meadow, oh! tell me, where is my mistress? --She has followed the banks of the stream.

--Beautiful river who just saw her passing, tell me, is she hereabouts? --She has left me to stray on the road. --Oh, road, do you still see her? --She has left me for the street.

--Oh, white street, path of the city, tell me, oh! where have you lead her? --To the golden street, which enters Sardis. --Oh! pathway of light, do her naked feet press you? --She has entered the home of the King.

--Oh, palace of splendor, light of the world, give her again back to me! --See! she has necklaces, hung to her breasts, chaplets of blossoms entwined in her hair, long strings of pearls looped on her legs, and two arms encircle her waist.

LYKAS

Come, we will stray in the fields, under the juniper bushes; we will eat honey fresh from the hive and make grasshopper traps from the daffodil stems.

Come, we'll see Lykas, who watches his father's flocks on the shadowy slopes of the Tauros. Surely he'll give us some milk.

I can hear his flute even now. He plays so cleverly. Here are the dogs and the lambs, and there he leans against a tree. Is he not even as fair as Adonis?

Oh, Lykas, give us some milk. Here are some figs from our trees. We have come to stay with you. Oh! bearded nannies, do not leap so high, lest you soon excite the restless goats.

OFFERING TO THE GODDESS

This garland plaited by my very hands is not for Artemis who rules at Perga--though Artemis will shield me from the labour-pangs.

Nor for Sidonian Athene, although she be of ivory and gold, and bears in her hand a pomegranate to tempt the birds.

No, but for Aphrodite whom I love within my breast, for she alone can sate my hungry lips if I suspend upon her sacred tree my loops of tender rosebuds.

But never will I say my need aloud. I'll stand on tiptoe, whispering my wish in secret to a crevice in the bark.

THE ACCOMMODATING FRIEND

The storm had lasted all night. Selenis of the lovely hair had come to spin with me. She stayed for fear of the mud, and, pressed tightly each to each, we filled my tiny bed.

When young girls sleep together sleep itself remains outside the door. "Bilitis, tell me, tell me whom you love." She slipped her thigh across my own to warm me sweetly.

And she whispered into my mouth: "I know, Bilitis, whom you love. Close your eyes, I am Lykas." I answered, touching her, "Can't I tell that you are just a girl? Your joke's a clumsy one."

But she went on: "Truly I am Lykas if you close your lids. Here are his arms, here are his hands" ... and tenderly, in the silence, she flushed my dreaming with a stranger dream.

PRAYER TO PERSEPHONE

Cleansed by the ritual ablutions and clothed in violet robes, we droop our olive branches to the earth.

"Oh, underworld Persephone, whatever be the name that thou desirest, if this name pleases thee, oh, hear our prayer, Crowned with Shadows, barren smile-less Queen!

"Koklis, daughter of Thrasymakos, is lying at thy door. Pray do not call her yet; thou knowest she cannot fly from thee for ever; but take her later, call some other day.

"Oh, bear her not away so soon, Invisible Mistress! For she bewails her virginity, she supplicates thee through our prayers; to save her we will give our three black sheep, unshorn."

GAME OF DICE

Since both of us adored him, we engaged to play a game of dice for him. That was a famous party. Many maidens watched most anxiously.

She led off with the Cyclops throw, and I cast the Solon. Then she threw Kallibolos, and I, sensing my defeat, besought the Goddess.

I played, I threw Epiphenon, she the high cast of Kios; I the Antiteukos and she the Trikias; and then I threw the cast of Aphrodite which wins the cherished lover.

The girl grew pale; I clasped her by the neck and whispered in her ear (that no one else might know), "Don't cry, my friend, we'll let him choose between us."

THE DISTAFF

All day my mother has shut me in the women's rooms, together with my sisters whom I loathe, who speak among themselves in lowered voice. In my own little corner, far away, I ply my distaff.

Distaff dear, since I'm alone with you, 'tis you alone who'll be my confidante. Your worsted wig of white makes you a woman. Hear me.

If I were able I should not be here, seated in the shadow of the wall and spinning boredly: I should be lain in violets upon the slopes of Tauros.

Since he is not as rich as I, my mother will not let him marry me. But let me tell you; either I will die before my wedding day; or he will be the one to lead me out...

THE FLUTE

For the Hyacinthian day he gave me some Panic pipes, of measured reeds well-cut, bound each to each with soft white wax, sweet as honey to my lips.

He teaches me to play, I seated on his knees; perhaps I tremble just a bit too much. He then plays after me in tones so sweet I scarce can hear them.

We did not have a word to tell each other, we were so close together all the time, but the songs we sang were answers to each other, and time again our mouths would seek the flute to find each other's there.

How late it is! the green night-frog commences now to sing. My mother never will believe I stayed so long to try to find the girdle that I lost.

TRESSES

[6]

He said to me: "Tonight I dreamed a dream.-- Your hair came down and fell about my throat. Your locks were as a yoke about my neck, a black fan spreading on my breast.

"And I caressed them; and they were my own; and we were bound together thus forever, by the same tresses, mouth on mouth, like two twin laurels with a single root.

"And little by little, it seemed to me, our limbs were so entwined that I became your body, or you entered into mine like some sweet dream mingling with my own."

When he had finished he softly placed his hands upon my shoulders, and looked into my eyes with such a look I lowered them and trembled...

THE GOBLET

Lykas saw me coming, clad only in a short and filmy shift, so torrid was the day; he wished to mould my breast, which was uncovered.

He took a handful of the finest clay, kneaded it in water, fresh and light. When he spread it gently on my skin, it was so cold I thought that I should faint.

Modeled from my breast he made a cup, rounded gently and umbilicate. He placed it in the burning sun to bake, and painted it with gold and purple paints, impressing flowers all about the rim.

Then we visited the spring which is sacred to the nymphs, and threw the goblet in the stream and strewed upon it gilly-flower stems.

ROSES IN THE NIGHT

After night creeps up the sky, the earth belongs to us and to the gods. We come from the fields to the brink of the stream; our bare feet guide us from the heavy-shadowed woods into the clearings.

Tiny stars shine brilliantly enough for the tiny shadows that we are. Sometimes we find a sleeping roe beneath the low-hung branches.

But that which is more beautiful at night than any other thing, is a place known only to ourselves which draws us through the fastness of the wood; a heavy bush of mysterious roses.

For no other touch of god-head upon earth can equal the scent of roses in the night. How is it that when I found myself alone I was not intoxicated by their smell?

REGRETS

At first I did not answer, shame sat upon my cheeks and the throbbing of my heart hurt my breasts.

Then I struggled, I said "No! no!". I turned my head, and the kiss did not meet my lips, nor did desire spread my close-locked knees.

He asked my pardon, kissed my hair, I felt his hot breath on me, and he left... Now I am alone.

I see the empty place, the lonely wood, the trampled earth. And I gnaw my fists till they bleed, and I stifle my sobs in the grass.

INTERRUPTED SLEEP

I fell asleep alone like a partridge in the heath...The light breeze, the noise of the water and the softness of the night had held me there.

I had fallen asleep, imprudently, and I awoke with a scream, and I struggled and I wept; but it was too late already. What service are a child's hands?

He would not leave me. Nay, he clasped me more fondly in his arms, pressed me against him and I saw no more, nor earth nor trees but only the glowing fire in his eyes.

To you, victorious Kypris, I consecrate these offerings, still moist with dew, vestiges of the anguish of a maid, witnesses of my slumber and my struggle.

TO THE WASHERWOMEN

Oh, washerwomen, do not say that you have seen me! I trust myself to you; do not betray me! Between my garment and my breasts, I bring you something to be washed.

I am like a little frightened hen... I cannot say just yet if I dare tell ... My beating heart may even kill me now ... I am bringing you a cloth.

A garment and the ribbons about my limbs. You see; there is some blood. By Apollo, it was in spite of me! I struggled hard enough; but men who love are stronger than we are.

Wash them well; spare neither salt nor chalk. I'll pledge four oboli for you at Aphrodite's feet; and even a silver drachma.

SONG

When he came back, I hid my face within my hands. He said: "Fear nothing. Who has seen our kiss? --Who saw us? The night and the moon."

"And the stars and the first flush of dawn. The moon has seen its visage in the lake, and told it to the water 'neath the willows. The water told it to the rower's oar.

"And the oar has told it to the boat, and the boat has passed the secret to the fisher. Alas! alas! if that were only all! But the fisher told the secret to a woman.

"The fisher told the secret to a woman: my father and my mother and my sisters, and all of Hellas now shall know the tale."

BILITIS

One woman drapes herself in snowy wool. Another clothes herself in silk and gold. And still another hangs herself with flowers, green leaves and purple grapes.

As for myself, I must live forever nude. My lover, come and take me as I am; without a dress or jewels or little boots, behold me! Bilitis herself and nothing more.

My hair is black from its blackness, and my lips are red from their red. My ringlets float about me free and loose and round as feathers.

Take me as my mother made me in a distant night of love, and if I please you in that fashion, please do not forget to tell me so.

THE COTTAGE

The little cottage where he has his bed is the loveliest on earth. It is made of the boughs of trees, four walls of sun-baked clay, and ringleted above with moss and sod.

I love him, for there we lie now that the nights are cool; and, the cooler the nights, the longer they become. At break of day I find that I am tired.

The mattress is upon the earth; two covers of black wool enclose our warming bodies. His chest is pressing hard against my breasts. My heart throbs...

He crushes me so hard that I shall break, frail little creature that I know I am; but once he is in me nothing else exists, and I could have my four limbs cut away without awakening from my ecstasy.

THE LOST LETTER

Alas, for me! for I have lost his letter. I had placed it 'twixt my skin and my strophion, [7] beneath the shielding warmth of my breast. I ran, it must have fallen out.

I shall return upon my homeward path; should someone find it he would tell my mother, and I'd be whipped before my mocking sisters.

If a man has found it he will give it to me; or even if he cares to speak to me in secret, I know the way to ravish him of it.

But should a woman once have gazed upon it, oh, Guardian Zeus protect me! for I know she'd tell the tale to everyone, or else I'm sure she'd steal my lover from me.

SONG

"The night is so deep that it creeps between my eyelids. --You will never find the path. You'll be lost within the wood.

--The noise of falling waters fills my ears. --You would not hear the murmurs of your lover though he should be but twenty steps away.

--The odor of the flowers is so strong that I shall faint and fall upon the path. --You would not feel him should he cross your road.

--Ah! though he is so far from here, across the very mountain, I see him and I hear him and I feel him touching me."

THE VOW

"When the waters of the river climb the snowy-covered peaks; when wheat and barley sprout between the moving ocean hills;

"When pine-trees take their birth from lakes and water-lilies spring from stones, and when the sun grows black and the moon falls on the grass;

"Then but then alone, shall I take another mistress, then shall I forget thee, Bilitis, soul of my life, heart of my heart."

He told me so! he told me so! What matters all the world,--where is the madder ecstasy to match itself beside my own!

NIGHT

And now 'tis I who seek him. Each night I softly steal from out the house, and travel by a long and devious path unto his meadow, there to watch him sleep.

Sometimes I stay a long time, never speaking, happy just to see him; just to kiss his breath I bend my lips unto his own.

Then suddenly I stretch myself upon him. He wakens in my arms and cannot rise, for I resist him. He scolds and laughs and tightly squeezes me. Thus do we play in the night.

... The blush of dawn, oh, naughty glow on the horizon, you already! Within what cave forever night, upon what meadow underneath the ground, shall we be able, wrapped in love, to love so long that we should soon forget the memory of you...

CRADLE SONG

Sleep. I have brought your baubles far from Sardis; your clothes from Babylon. Sleep on: daughter of Bilitis and a king of the rising sun.

The woods, these are the palaces that have been built for you--that I have given. The trunks of pine-trees are your colonnades; the branches flying high upon the air, your vaulted ceiling.

Sleep. I'll sell the sunlight to the heaving sea that it may not awaken you. Your breath is lighter than the breeze stirred by the wings of snowy doves.

Daughter of mine, flesh of my flesh, you'll tell me when you waken if you wish the city or the meadow, the mountain or the moon, or just the white procession of the gods.

THE TOMB OF THE NAÏADS

I walked through the frost-encrusted wood; my hair blossomed with tiny icicles before my mouth and my sandals were heavy with soiled and caked-up snow.

He said to me: "What do you seek?"--"I follow the tracks of the satyr. His little cleft foot-prints alternate like holes in a snow-white robe." He said to me: "The satyrs are dead.

"The satyrs, and the nymphs also. For thirty years there has not been so terrible a winter. The tracks you see are those of a goat. But stay here, here is their tomb."

And with the iron of his hoe he broke the ice of the spring in which the naïads were wont to laugh of yore. He took some of the great frozen chunks, and, raising them to the pale heavens, looked through them.

[1] The Greek, as translated by R. C. Trevelyan in his edition of the *Idylls of Theocritus* published by the Casanova Society, 1925, reads (XX-28-2-9):
"Sweet is my music too, whether I warble on the pipe, Or discourse on the flute, or on the reed or flageolet."
[2] *From his white horses' backs*: There are so many variations of the classic myths that this might well apply to Phaeton, although it does not matter either way.

[3] *Amalthea*: a mythical figure, varying according to the legend, from a goat to a nymph to the daughter of a Cretan king, all attributed with having nursed or tended the infant Zeus in Crete.

[4] *Sparrow*: I have not hesitated to change the French "*Bergeronette*" into a sparrow, the usual translation of the birds which drew Aphrodite's car. Although the actual bird was probably some species of finch, a qualifying adjective is needed, for the Greek "sparrow" was not the pestiferous British bird with which we are acquainted.

Kypris ... or *Cypris* (Aphrodite) also known as *Paphia* (vide p. 69). Aphrodite's innumerable epithets and appellations, excluding her purely national names, such as *Venus*, *Aphrodite*, *Astarte*, *Tanit*, etc., were largely derived from the names of the various towns at which she had her shrines Paphos, Cyprus, etc. In the text itself I have adhered to Louÿs' Greek spelling, with the exception of those words whose appearance might be confusing to readers unacquainted with classical terminology.

[5] *little Helle met her death*: by falling off the back of the ram which bore the Golden Fleece. This much sought-after beast had been loaned to the mother of Helle (Nephele) by Mercury, to facilitate the escape of Helle and her brother Phryxus from the influence of their father, who was a King in Thessaly. The Hellespont took its name from the spot "Where beauteous Helle found a watery grave. " (Meleager).

[6] Tresses: Here an apology is due, for the necessity of translating *Chevelure* as *tresses*. I can find no other word, hair, locks, or ringlets, which will express the word better than the hackneyed *tresses*.

[7] *strophion*: a sort of ancient *brassière*, or sash about the breast.

II - Elegies at Mytilene

Εὐμορφοτέρα Μνασιδίκα τᾶς ἀπαλᾶς Γυρινν῵ς.
SAPPHO

[1]

TO THE SHIP

Lovely ship that bore me here, skirting the coast of the Ionic sea, I leave you to the gleaming waves again and with a light step leap upon the strand.

You are returning to the distant land, where the virgin is companion to the nymphs. Do not forget to thank the unseen counsellors and carry them this bough, plucked by my hands.

You were a pine-tree standing on the hills; your spiny branches, squirrels and your birds all trembled in the angry Notos [2] blast.

May Boreas guide you now, and press you gently onward to the port, black vessel companioned by the dolphins, at the mercy of the ever-watchful sea.

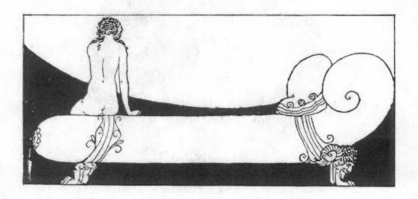

PSAPPHA

I rub my eyes. it is already day, I think. Ah! who is by my side? ... a woman? ... By Paphia, [3] I had forgotten! ... Oh, Charites! how hot with shame I am!

To what country have I come, what isle is this, where love is comprehended in this fashion? If I were not so tired, I should think I had been dreaming ... Can it be that this is Psappha?

She sleeps ... She certainly is beautiful, although her hair is cut in virile fashion. But this strange face, this mannish bosom and these narrow hips...

I had best leave before she wakens. Alas! I am lying by the wall. I must step over her. I am afraid to brush against her hip, afraid that she might try to hold me back.

THE DANCE OF GLOTTIS AND KYSE

Two little girls had led me to their home, and as soon as the door was closed they touched the wick unto the fire and wished to dance for me.

Their unrouged cheeks were tan, just like their little bellies. They grasped each other by the arms and chattered joyously.

Seated upon a raised and padded trestle, Glottis sang in a sharp voice, and struck her noisy little hands together.

Kyse danced in quick staccato fashion, then stopping, winded with laughter, grasped her sister by her breasts, bit her shoulder and turned her roundabout much like a playful goat.

COUNSELS

Then Syllikmas entered, and, seeing that we were so intimate, sat down upon the bench. Taking Glottis on one knee and Kyse on the other, she began:

"Come here, my dear." But I remained away. Then she went on: "Are you afraid of us? Come closer: these children truly love you. They can teach you things you do not know about: the honey-like caresses of a girl.

"Man is violent and lazy. You doubtless know him well. Then hate him. He has a flattened breast, rough skin, short hair and shaggy arms. But women are entirely beautiful.

"And only women know the art of love; stay with us, Bilitis, do stay. And if you have a truly ardent spirit, you'll see your beauty as within a glass upon the bodies of your mistresses."

INCERTITUDE

I do not know if I shall mate myself with Glottis or with Kyse. As they are not much alike, one cannot soothe me for the other's loss, and greatly fear to make an evil choice.

Each has one of my hands, and one of my breasts too. To which I wonder shall I give my mouth? to which my heart, and all one cannot share?

For it is shameful to stay this way, all three within one house. They talk of such things here in Mytilene. Yesterday before the temple of Ares a passing woman did not say "Good-day"

'Tis Glottis I prefer; but I cannot disown Kyse. What would become of her all by herself? Or shall I leave them together as I found them, and take another lover for my-self?

MEETING

I found her as a treasure, in a field, under a myrtle bush; she was wrapped from throat to feet in a yellow peplos broidered fine with blue.

"I have no lover," she told me, "for the nearest town is forty stadia [4] from here. I live alone but for my mother, who is a widow and is always sad. If you should wish me I would follow you.

"I'll follow to your house, though it should be upon the other sea-coast of the isle; and I'll live with you until you send me hence. Your hand is tender and your eyes are blue.

"Let us go. I'll carry nothing with me but the little nude Astarte which is hanging from my necklace. We'll place it close to yours, and reward them with red roses every night."

THE LITTLE CLAY ASTARTE

The little guardian Astarte which protects Mnasidika, was modeled at Camiros by a very clever potter. She is as large as your thumb, of fine-ground yellow clay.

Her tresses fall and circle about her narrow shoulders. Her eyes are cut quite widely and her mouth is very small. For she is the All-Beautiful.

Her right hand indicates her delta, which is peppered with tiny holes about her lower belly and along her groins. For she is the All-Lovable.

Her left hand supports her round and heavy breasts. Between her spreading hips swings a large and fertile belly. For she is the Mother-of-All.

DESIRE

She entered, and passionately, with half-closed eyes, she joined her lips with mine, and our tongues knew each other... Never in my life had there been a kiss like that.

She stood against me, amorous and willing. Little by little my knee rose between her warm thighs, which spread as though receptive to a lover.

My wandering hand upon her gown sought her secret body, which alternately swayed in undulation, or arching, stiffened with tremblings of the skin.

With maddened eyes she looked upon the bed; but we had no right to love before the wedding, and we separated hastily at last.

THE WEDDING

The wedding feast was given in the morning, in Acalanthis' house whom she had taken for a mother. Mnasidika wore a milk-white veil, and I the virile tunic.

Then after, in the midst of twenty women she donned her festal robes. Perfumed with bakkaris and spread with gold-dust, her cool and rippling skin attracted furtive hands.

In her leafy chamber she awaited me, as a bridegroom. And I led her out in a little two-wheeled cart, seated between me and the nymphagogue. [5] One of her little breasts burned in my hand.

They sang the nuptial song: the flutes sang madly. And carrying Mnasidika, my arms beneath her knees and round her shoulders, I passed the threshold, strewn with blushing roses.

THE LIVING PAST

I left the bed as she had left it, unmade and rumpled, coverlets awry, so that her body's print might rest still warm beside my own.

Until the next day I did not go to bathe, I wore no clothes and did not dress my hair, for fear I might erase some sweet caress.

That morning I did not eat, nor yet at dusk, and put no rouge nor powder on my lips, so that her kiss might cling a little longer.

I left the shutters closed, and did not open the door, for fear the memory of the might before might vanish with the wind.

METAMORPHOSIS

I formerly was amorous of the beauty of young men, and the memory of their words, one time, would keep me long awake.

I remember having carved a name in the bark of a sycamore. I remember having left a fragment of my gown upon the road where one was wont to pass.

I remember having loved... Oh! Pannychis, my child, in what hands have I left you? How could I, unhappy one, have thus abandoned you?

Today Mnasidika alone possesses me, and will forever have me. Let her receive as sacrifice the happiness of those whom I have left for her.

THE NAMELESS TOMB

Mnasidika then took me by the hand, and led me through the portals of the town to a little barren field where a marble shaft was standing. She said to me: "This was my mother's mistress."

I felt a sudden tremor, and, clinging to her hand, leaned on her shoulder, to read the four verses between the serpent and the broken bowl:

"Death did not carry me away, but the Nymphs of the river. I rest here beneath the light earth with the shorn ringlets of my Xantho. Let her alone weep for me. I shall not say my name."

We stood there long and did not pour libation. How can one call upon an unknown soul from out the rushing hordes of souls in Hades?

MNASIDIKA'S THREE BEAUTIES

That Mnasidika may be protected by the gods, I sacrificed two doves and two male hares to laughter-loving Aphrodite.

To Ares [6] I have given two armed cocks, and sinister Hecate has received two dogs who howled beneath the knife.

Nor have I wrongly prayed these three immortals, for Mnasidika bears upon her face the imprint of their trinal godhead:

Her lips are red as copper, her hair shines blue as steel and her eyes are black as silver.

THE GROTTO OF THE NYMPHS

Your little feet are daintier than those of silver Thetis. [7] You cross your arms and press your breasts together, and rock them softly, like two snowy doves.

Beneath your hair you hide your moistened eyes, your trembling mouth and the red flowers of your ears; but naught shall stay my gentle glance or the warm breath of my kiss.

For in the secret of your body it is you, beloved Mnasidika, who hide the grotto of the nymphs which aged Homer sings, the place where the naïads weave their purple robes.

Where drop by drop the quenchless springs do flow, and from which the Northern gate permits men to descend, and where the South Gate lets Immortals enter.

MNASIDIKA'S BREASTS

Carefully, with one hand, she opened her tunic and tendered me her breasts, warm and sweet, just as one offers the goddess a pair of living turtle-doves.

"Love them well," she said to me, "I love them so! They are little darlings, little children. I busy myself with them when I am alone. I play with them; I pleasure them.

WILLY POGANY

"I flush them with milk. I powder them with flowers. I dry them with my fine-spun hair, soft to their little nipples. I caress them and I shiver. I couch them in soft wool.

"Since I shall never have a child, be their nursling, oh! my love, and since they are so distant from my mouth, kiss them, sweet, for me."

THE DOLL

I have given her a doll, a waxen doll with rosy cheeks. Its arms are attached by little pins, and even its little legs can bend.

When we are together she places it between us in the bed; it is our child. At eventide she rocks it and gives it the breast before putting it to sleep.

She has woven it three little tunics, and on the Aphrodisian days we give it little jewels, jewels and also flowers.

She is careful of its virtue, and will not let it out alone; especially in the sun, for the little doll would melt and drip away in drops of wax.

TENDERNESS

Softly clasp your arms, like a girdle, about me. Touch, oh, touch my skin like that again! Neither water nor the noon-time breeze is gentle as your hand.

Today you shall fondle me, little sister; 'tis your turn. Remember the caresses that I taught you last night, and kneel beside me who am tired, and do not say a word.

Your lips sink from my lips. And all your unbound ring-lets follow them, as the caress follows fast upon the kiss. They fall upon my left breast; they hide your eyes from me.

Give me your hand, it is so warm! Press mine and do not leave it. Hands join with hands more easily than mouth with mouth, and nothing can compare with their passion.

GAMES

More than her baubles and her doll am I a plaything for Mnasidika. For hours on end, unspeaking, like a child, she amuses herself with all my body's charms.

She undoes my hair and does it up again according to her fancy, sometimes knotting it beneath my chin like some heavy cloth, or twisting it into a knot behind my neck, or plaiting it until its very end.

She looks with wonder at the color of my lashes, or on the bending of my elbow-joint. Sometimes she places me on hands and knees:

And then (it is one of her games), she slips her little head underneath, and plays the trembling kid at nursing time beneath its mother's belly.

SHADOWLIGHT

We slipped beneath the transparent coverlet of wool, she and I. Even our heads were hidden, and the lamp lit up the cloth above us.

And thus I saw her dear body in a mysterious glow. We were much closer to each other, freer, more naked and more intimate. "In the selfsame shift," she said to me.

We left our hair done up so that we'd be more bare, and in the close air of the bed two female odors rose, as from two natural censers.

Nothing in the world, not even the lamp, saw us that night. And which of us was loved and which the lover, she and I alone can ever tell. But the men shall never know a thing about it.

THE SLEEPER

She sleeps in her undone hair, her hands entwined behind her neck. But does she dream? Her lips are parted and her breath is gentle.

With a little dab of down I dry, without awakening her, the perspiration from her arms, the fever from her cheeks. Her closed eyelids are two purple flowers.

I shall arise quietly; I'll go draw water, milk the cow, and beg some fire from our neighbors. I want to be coiffed and dressed completely when she opens her eyes.

Sleep, remain awhile between her lovely curving lashes, and spin out the happy night with a dream of happy omen.

THE KISS

I shall kiss from end to end the long black wings spreading from your neck, oh, gentle bird, captive dove whose heart throbs wild beneath my hand!

I shall take your mouth into my mouth as the child takes its mother's breast. Tremble! for the kiss sinks deep and should suffice for love.

I shall trail my light tongue along your arms and round your neck, and I shall drag the long drawn kiss of my nails along your tender sides.

Hear roaring in your ear all the murmur of the sea... Mnasidika! the expression of your eyes makes me ill. I'll clasp within my kiss your lids which burn as warmly as your lips.

JEALOUS CARES

You must not dress your hair for fear the iron might burn your neck or singe your lovely locks. You'll let it rest upon your shoulders, and spread along your arms.

You must not dress yourself, for fear your girdle might redden the fine-drawn lines about your hips. Remain naked like a little girl.

You must not even rise, for fear your tender feet might become sore with walking here and there. You shall remain in bed, oh Eros' prey, and I shall dress your wound!

For I would not see upon your body any other mark, Mnasidika, than the mark of a kiss too long-impressed, the scratch of a sharpened nail, or the purpled bar of my own embrace.

THE MAD EMBRACE

Love me, not with smiles and flutes or plaited flowers, but with your heart and tears, as I adore you with my bosom and my sobs.

When your breasts alternate with mine, when I feel your very life touching my own, when your knees rise up behind me, my panting mouth no longer even knows the way to yours.

Clasp me as I clasp you! See, the lamp has just gone out, we toss about in the night; but I press your moving body and I hear your ceaseless plaint...

Moan! moan! moan! oh, woman! Eros drags us now in heavy pain. You'll suffer less upon this bed in bringing forth a child than you'll agonize in bringing forth your love.

THE HEART

Panting, I took her hand and pressed it tightly beneath the humid skin of my left breast. My head tossed here and there and I moved my lips, but not a word escaped.

My maddened heart, sudden and hard, beat and beat upon my breast, as a captive satyr would beat about, tied in a goat-skin vessel. She said to me: "Your heart is troubling you..."

"Oh, Mnasidika!" I answered her, "a woman's heart is not seated *there*. This is but a little bird, a dove which stirs its feeble wings. The heart of a woman is more terrible.

"It burns like a myrtle-berry, with a bright red flame and beneath abundant foam. 'Tis there that I feel bitten by voracious Aphrodite."

NIGHT WORDS

We are resting, our eyes closed; the quietude is great about our bed. Ineffable summer nights! But she, thinking that I sleep, puts her warm hand on my arm.

She murmurs: "Bilitis, are you asleep?" My heart pounds, but without answering I breathe as calmly as a sleeping woman in her dreams. Then she begins to speak:

"Since you cannot hear me," she says, "Ah! how I love you!" And she repeats my name: "Bilitis ... Bilitis ... " And she strokes me with the tips of trembling fingers:

"This mouth is mine! and mine alone! Is there another in the world as lovely? Ah! my happiness, my happiness! These naked arms are mine, this neck, this hair..."

ABSENCE

She has gone out, and she is far away, but I see her still, for all within this room is full of her, all is hers, and I just like the rest.

This bed, still warm, where my mouth is wandering now, is rumpled to the pattern of her body. In this soft pillow her little ringleted head has softly slept.

This is the basin where she oft has washed; this comb has smoothed the knots of her tangled hair. These slippers have held her little naked feet. This gauze bandeau restrained her swelling breasts.

But I dare not touch, even with my finger, this mirror in which she sees her burning bruises, and in which, perhaps, the image of her sweet moist lips is still reflected.

LOVE

Alas! if I think of her my throat is parched, my head is drooped, my breasts grow hard and make me ill at case, I tremble and I weep the while I walk.

If I see her my heart stops, my hands shake, my feet grow cold and fire mounts in my checks, while my temples pulse sadly on and on.

If I touch her I grow mad, my arms stiffen and my knees grow weak. I fall before her and curl up like a woman wont to die.

I am hurt by everything she says to me. Her love is like a torture, and the passers-by can hear my constant plaint... Alas! how can I call her Well-Beloved?

PURIFICATION

There you are! Undo your bandelettes, your clasps and tunic. Undress right to your sandals, down to the ribbons twined about your legs, down to the cincture bound about your breast.

Sponge the black from your brows and the rouge from your lips. Wash the whiting from your shoulders and unroll your knotted tresses in the water.

For I want you pure, such as you were born upon the bed, at the feet of your fertile mother and before your noble sire.

So chaste that my hand within your hand will make you blush to the lips, and a whispered word of mine within your ear will madden your rolling eyes.

MNASIDIKA'S LULLABY

My little child, as few years older as I am than you, I love you, not as a lover loves, but as though you had come forth from my womb in labour.

When, stretched upon my knees, frail arms about my neck, you seek my breast, and with mouth held forward you slowly suck with palpitating lips,

I dream that at some former time I really nursed this supple, wet and tender mouth, this purple vase of myrrh in which my happiness is mysteriously enclosed.

Sleep! I'll cradle you upon my rocking knee with one hand. Sleep, so. I'll sing you mournful little songs, songs used to lull the new-born child to sleep.

SEA-SIDE PROMENADE

As we were walking on the shore, unspeaking, wrapped to the chin in our dark woolen robes, some happy young girls passed by.

"Ah! it's Bilitis and Mnasidika! See the lovely little squirrel that we caught: it is soft as a bird and frightened as a rabbit.

"At Lydia's house we'll put it in a cage, and give it lots of milk and salad-leaves. It's female, and will live a long, long time."

And the mad little creatures ran along. But we, un-speaking, sat upon the beach, I on a rock and she upon the sand, and we looked far out to sea.

THE OBJECT

Hail Bilitis, Mnasidika hail. --Sit down. How is your hus-band? --Much too well. Do not tell him that you have seen me. He'd kill me if he knew that I was here. --You need not fear.

--And there is your room? and there your bed? I beg your pardon. I am curious. --You know Myrrhina's bed, however. --So little. --They say it's pretty. --And lascivious; oh, my dear! but I must keep quiet.

--What do you wish of me? --That you lend me... --Speak. -- I dare not name the object. --We have none. --Truly? --Mnasidika is a virgin. --Well, where can one be bought? --At Drako, the harness--maker's.

--Tell me, too, who sells you your embroidery thread? Mine breaks if you even look at it. -- I make my own, but Naïs sells good thread. --At what price? --Three oboli. --That's dear. And the object? --Two drachmae. --Farewell.

EVENING BY THE FIRE

The winter is severe, Mnasidika. Everything is cold outside our bed. Arise, however; come with me, for I have built a great fire of dead logs and split kindling wood.

We will crouch down and warm ourselves, quite nude, our hair hung down our backs, and drink milk out of the self-same cup and munch on honeyed cakes.

How sonorous and gay the fire is! Are you not too near? Your skin is getting red. Let me kiss it wherever the fire has made it hot.

I'll warm the iron amidst the burning brands and dress your hair right here. And with a burnt-out coal I'll write your name upon the wall.

PRAYERS

What do you want? Say it. If you should wish I'll sell my last jewel, so that a watchful slave may wait upon the wishes of your eyes, upon whatever thirst your lips may have.

If our goat's milk should seem flat to you, I'll hire, as for a child, a wet-nurse with great swollen breasts to suckle you each morning of the year.

If our bed should be too hard upon your back, I'll purchase all the puffy pillows, all the silken coverlets, and all the Amathusian merchants' cloths, furred with feathers.

All. But I myself must also fill your need, and if we sleep upon the earth, the earth must be much softer to your back than the comfortable bed of any stranger.

EYES

Mnasidika's great eyes, how you delight me when desire darkens your lids and fires you and drowns you in its tears!

How wild you make me when you turn aside, distracted by some passing lovely girl, or by a memory which is not my own.

Then my cheeks grow hollow, my hands tremble and I suffer... It seems to me my life blood slips away, before your eyes, from every part of me.

Mnasidika's great eyes, oh, do not cease to feast yourselves on me! or I'll prick you with my needle, and you'll see nothing but the dreadful night.

COSMETICS

Everything, my life and all the world., and men, all that is not she, is naught. All that is not she, I give you, passer-by.

Does she know how many tasks I accomplish to be lovely in her eyes, tasks with my coiffure and my paints, my dresses and my perfumes?

Just so long would I tread the mill, or pull the oar or even till the soil, if these would be the price of holding her.

But never let her know these things, oh, guardian Goddesses! The very day she knows that I adore her, she'll seek another woman.

MNASIDIKA'S SILENCE

All day she laughed and even mocked at me a little. She refused to obey me, in the presence of some strangers.

When we had come home again I affected not to speak to her, and when she threw her arms about my neck, saying: "Are you angry?" I said to her:

"Ah! you are no longer as you used to be, you are no longer like the first day. I do not recognize you any more, Mnasidika." She did not answer me.

But she put on all her jewels, the jewels that she had not worn for long, and even the blue-embroidered yellow robe she had not worn since the day of our first meeting.

SCENE

Where were you? --At the florist's. I bought some lovely irises. Behold them, I have brought them just for you. --And you took all that time to buy four flowers? --The merchant kept me waiting.

--Your cheeks are pale, and your eyes are shining. --The weariness of walking such away. --Your hair is wet and tangled. --The heat is great, the wind has tossed my hair.

--Your girdle was untied. I made the knot myself, and not as hard as that. --So loose it opened; a passing slave tied it up for me.

--There is a spot on your dress. --The flowers dripped. --Mnasidika, my little soul, your irises are far more beautiful than can be bought in all of Mytilene. --How well I know it, oh, how well I know!

WAITING

The sun spent all the night in the country of the dead, while I have waited, seated on my bed, fatigued from having stayed so long awake. The wick of the exhausted lamp has burned until the end.

She will not come: there is the last star. How well I know that she will come no more. I even know the very name I hate. And still I wait.

Let her come now! yes, let her come, her hair undone, ungarlanded, her dresses soiled and spotted, rumpled up, her tongue dry and her eyelids black!

As soon as she opens the door I'll say to her ... but there she is... It is her dress I touch, her hands, her hair, her skin! I kiss her with a maddened mouth, and weep.

SOLITUDE

For whom shall I rouge my lips now? For whom shall I polish my nails? For whom perfume my hair?

For whom shall I rub my breasts with rouge, if they can no longer tempt her? For whom shall I flush my arms with milk, if they never again can hold her!

How shall I be able to sleep? How shall I get to bed? To-night my hand, in all the bed, has not found her own warm hand.

I dare no longer enter my home, into the room, frightfully bare. I no longer dare open the door again. I never dare open my eyes.

LETTER

This is impossible, impossible. I beg you on my knees, in tears, all the tears that I have wept upon this dreadful letter; do not abandon me this way.

Think of how dreadful it is to lose you forever, for the second time, after having had the immense joy of hoping to recapture you. Ah! my loves, do you not feel to what extreme I love you!

Listen to me. Consent to see me just once more. Will you be, tomorrow, at the setting of the sun, before your door? Tomorrow, or the next day. I shall come to get you. Do not refuse me that.

The last time, perhaps; so be it, but just this time, just this one time more! I ask it of you, beg it of you, and think that the remainder of my life hangs on your answer.

ATTEMPT

You were jealous of us, Gyrinno, over-ardent girl. How many garlands have you had suspended upon the knocker of our door! You waited for our passing and you followed us in the street.

Now you have attained your wish, stretched in the beloved place, your head upon the pillow where the odor of another woman clings. You are taller than she was. Your different body astonishes me.

See, I have finally yielded. Yes, 'tis L You may fondle my breasts, caress my belly, spread my willing knees. All my body is given to your quenchless, tireless lips--alas!

Ah, Gyrinno! my eyes, too, overflow with love. Dry them with your tresses but do not kiss them, oh, my sweet; and hold me tighter to overcome the trembling of my frame.

EFFORT

More! enough of sighing and stretching out your arms! Begin again! Or do you think that love is relaxation? Gyrinno, 'tis a task, and by far the most severe.

Awaken! You must not go to sleep! What matters to me your purple eyelids and the streak of pain which burns your slender legs. Astarte boils and bubbles in my loins.

We went to bed before twilight. Here already is the naughty dawn; but I am not so easily fatigued. I shall not sleep before the second night.

I shall not sleep: you *must* not go to sleep. Ah! how bitter is the taste of dawn! Gyrinno, judge of it! Kisses are more difficult, but stranger, longer, slow.

TO GYRINNO

Do not think that I have loved you. I have eaten you like a ripe fig, and drunk you like a draught of burning water, and worn you about me like a girdle of flesh.

I have amused myself with you, because you have short hair and pointed breasts upon your slender body, and nipples black as little dates.

As one must have fruits and water, a woman also sates a living thirst; but already I no longer know your name, you who have lain within my arms like the shade of another loved one.

Between your flesh and mine a burning dream has claimed me for its own. I pressed you on me as upon a wound, and cried: "Mnasidika! Mnasidika! Mnasidika!"

LAST ATTEMPT

What do you want, old girl? --To console you. --'Tis wasted effort. --I have been told that since your quarrel, you've gone from love to love, but have never found for-getfulness or peace. I come to suggest some one to you.

--Speak. --She is a young slave born in Sardis. She has not her equal in the world, for she is both man and wom-an, although her breast and long hair and clear voice are most deceptive.

--Her age? --Sixteen. --Her height? --Tall. She has known no one here excepting Psappha, who is madly in love with her and wished to buy her from me for twenty minae. If you should hire her, then she is yours. --What shall I do about it?

For twenty-two nights I've tried in vain to flee from memory... So be it; I'll take this one more, but warn the dear that she should not be frightened if I sob within her arms.

RENDING MEMORY

I remember ... (at what hour of the day is she not before my eyes!). I remember the way She had of lifting her hair with pale and dainty fingers.

I remember a night she passed, cheek against my breast, so sweetly that happiness kept me long awake; and the next day she had the imprint of the nipple on her face.

I see her holding her cup of milk, and looking at me sidewise with a smile. I see her, powdered and with her hair new-dressed, opening her great eyes before her mir-ror and touching up the rouge upon her lips.

And above all, if my despair is everlasting torture, it is because I know, minute by minute, how she trembles in the other's arms, and what she asks of her and what she gives, herself.

THE WAX DOLL

Wax-doll, dear plaything that she called her child, she has left you too and forgets you, like myself, who was with her your father or your mother, I forget.

The pressure of her lips has worn the paint from your little cheeks; and, on your left hand, here is the broken finger that made her cry so much. This little cyclas that you wear, 'twas, she who worked it for you.

According to her you could already read. However, you had not been weaned, and at night, leaning over you, she opened her tunic and gave you the breast, "so that you would not cry," she used to say.

Doll, if I should care to see her, I would give you to Aphrodite as the dearest of my gifts. But I want to think that she is wholly dead.

FUNERAL CHANT

Sing a funeral song, Mytilenian muses, sing! The earth is dark like a mourning cloak, and the yellow trees are trembling like tresses that are shorn.

Heraïos! oh, sad and gentle month! the leaves fall gently as the falling snow, the sun-beams are much stronger in the naked forest dells... I hear no longer anything but silence.

Here Pittakos, borne down with years, was carried to his tomb. Many whom I used to know are dead. And she who lives is as though she were no more, to me.

This is the tenth autumn I have watched dying on this land. It is time for me also to die. Weep with me, Mytilenian muses, weep upon my footprints in the earth!

[1] The Greek quotation, as translated by Wharton in his *Sappho, memoir, text, selected renderings*, Brentano, 1920, reads (p. 94): "Mnasidica is more shapely than the tender Gyrinno." Cf. the Life of Bilitis, p. 17.

[2] *Notos*: the south-west wind, bringing fog and rain. *Boreas*: the north wind.

[3] *Paphia*: see above, 33. *Charites*: the Graces, "goddesses of everything that lends charm and beauty to human life." (Harper's Dictionary of Classical Antiquity).

[4] *forty stadia*: about four and a half miles.

[5] *nymphagogue*: the matron who accompanied the bride to her husband's home.

[6] *Ares*: the Greek Mars. *Hecate*: a Titan, variously and loosely identified with Selene (the Moon), Artemis (Diana) and Persephone, but generally accepted as one of the underworld deities.

[7] *Thetis*: a fabulously beautiful nymph, originally sought after by the perennially potent Zeus, but destined to be the mother of Achilles, by a mortal, in order (rather equivocally) to fulfil the prophecy that he would be a greater man than his father.

III - Epigrams in the Isle of Cyprus

Ἀλλά με ναρκίσσοις ἀναδήσατε, καὶ πλαγιαύλων
γεύσατε καὶ κροκίνοις χρίσατε γυῖα μύροις.
Καὶ Μυτιληναίῳ τὸν πνεύμονα τέγξατε Βάκχῳ
καὶ συζεύξατέ μοι φωλάδα παρθενικήν.
PHILODEMUS

[1]

HYMN TO ASTARTE

Mother inexhaustible and incorruptible, creatures, born the first, engendered by thyself and by thyself conceived, issue of thyself alone and seeking joy within thyself, Astarte!

Oh! perpetually fertilized, virgin and nurse of all that is, chaste and lascivious, pure and revelling, ineffable, nocturnal, sweet, breather of fire, foam of the sea!

Thou who accordest grace in secret, thou who unitest, thou who lovest, thou who seizest with furious desire the multiplied races of savage beasts and couplest the sexes in the wood.

Oh, irresistible Astarte! hear me, take me, possess me, oh, Moon! and thirteen times each year draw from my womb the sweet libation of my blood!

HYMN TO THE NIGHT

The midnight masses of the trees move no more than do the mountains. The stars are crowded in a spreading sky. A breeze warm as a human breath caresses my cheeks and eyes.

Oh! Night who gave birth to the Gods! how sweet thou art upon my lips! how warm thou art in my hair! how thou enterest into me this evening, and I feel that I am big with all thy spring!

The flowers which are going to bloom will take their birth from me. The wind which breathes so softly is my breath. The wafted perfume is my own desire. All the living stars are in my eyes.

Thy voice, is it the murmur of the sea, or is it the silence of the fields? Thy voice, I do not understand it, but it dizzies me, and my tears bathe both my hands.

THE MAENADS

Through the forests that overhang the sea, the Maenads madly rushed. Maskale of the fiery breasts, howling, brandished the sycamore phallos, smeared with red.

All leaped and ran and cried aloud beneath their robes and crowns of twisted vine, crotals clacking in their hands, and thyrses splitting the bursting skins of echoing dulcimers.

With sopping hair and agile limbs, breasts reddened and tossed about, sweat of cheeks and foam of lips, oh, Dionysos! they offered in return the love that you had poured in them.

And the sea-wind tossed Heliokomis' russet hair unto the sky, and whipped it into a furious flame on her body's white-wax torch.

THE SEA OF KYPRIS

I had crouched on the edge of the highest promontory. The sea was black as a field of violets. And the Milky Way was gushing from the great supernal breast.

About me a thousand Maenads slept in the torn-up flowers. Long grasses mingled with their flowing hair. And now the sun was born from the eastern waters.

These the same waves and these the self-same shores that saw one day the white body of Aphrodite rising... I suddenly hid my eyes in my hands.

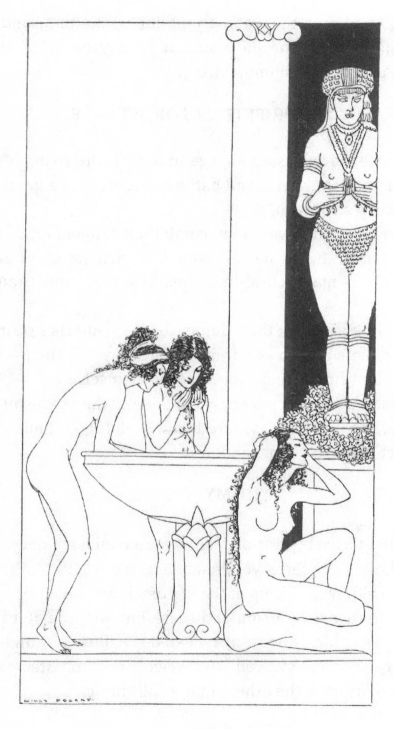

For I had seen the water trembling with a thousand little lips of light: the pure sex, or it may have been the smile of Kypris Philommeïdes. [2]

THE PRIESTESSES OF ASTARTE

Astarte's priestesses engage in love at the rising of the moon; then they arise and bathe themselves in a great basin with a silver rim.

With crook'd fingers they comb their tangled locks, and their purple-tinted hands twined in their jet-black curls are like so many coral-branches in a dark and running sea.

They never pluck their deltas, for the goddess's triangle marks their bellies as a temple; but they tint themselves with paint-brush, and heavily scent themselves.

Astarte's priestesses engage in love at the setting of the moon, then in a tent where burns a high gold lamp they stretch themselves at random.

THE MYSTERIES

[3]

In the thrice mysterious hall where men have never entered, we have fêted you, Astarte of the Night. Mother of the World, Well-Spring of the life of all the Gods!

I shall reveal a portion of the rite, but no more of it than is permissible. About a crowned Phallos, a hundred-twenty women swayed and cried. The initiates were dressed as men, the others in the split tunic.

The fumes of perfumes and the smoke of torches float-ed fog-like in and out among us all. I wept my scorching tears. All, at the feet of Berbeia, we threw ourselves, ex-tended on our backs.

Then, when the Religious Act was consummated, and when into the Holy Triangle the purpled phallos had been plunged anew, the mysteries began; but I shall say no more.

EGYPTIAN COURTESANS

I went with Plango to the Egyptian courtesans, far above the old city. They have amphoras of earth and cop-per salvers, and yellow mats on which they may squat without an effort.

Their rooms are silent, without angles or corners, so greatly have successive coats of blue white-wash softened the capitals and rounded off the bottoms of the walls.

They sit unmoving, hands upon their knees. When they offer porridge they murmur: "Happiness." And when one thanks them they say, "Thanks to you."

They understand Hellenic, but feign to speak it poorly so that they may laugh at us in their own tongue; but we, tooth for tooth, speak Lydian and they suddenly grow restless.

I SING MY FLESH AND MY LIFE

Certainly I shall not sing of celebrated mistresses. For, if they live no longer, why speak of them at all? Am I not quite similar to them? Have I not enough to do to think about myself?

I shall forget you, Pasiphaë, [4] although your passion was extreme. I shall not praise you, Syrinx, nor you, Byblis, nor you, white-armed Helen, goddess-chosen from among them all!

If one has suffered, I can scarcely feel it. If one has loved, I love more than she. I sing my flesh and my life, and not the sterile shades of buried lovers.

Stay softly couched, oh, my body, according to your voluptuous mission! Taste daily joys and passions whose tomorrow never comes. Leave no pleasure unexplored, lest you regret the evening of your death.

PERFUMES

[5]

I shall scent my skin all over to attract my lovers. Over my lovely limbs, in a silver basin, I'll pour the spikenard of Tarsos and metopion of Egypt.

Beneath my arms, some crisped mint; upon my lashes and my eyes, sweet-marjoram of Kôs. Slave, undo my hair, and fill it with the smoke of burning incense.

Here is oïnanthinon from the mountains of Kypros; I'll let it run between my heavy breasts; rose-liquor shipped from Phaselis will bathe my neck and cheeks.

And now spread on my loins some irresistible bakkaris. It is better for a courtesan to know the Lydian perfumes than the customs of the Peloponnesus.

CONVERSATION

Good-day. --Good-day to you. --You are in a hurry. --Perhaps less in a hurry than you think.

--You are a pretty girl. --Perhaps more pretty than you even know.

--What is your charming name? --I do not tell my name in such a hurry. --Have you some one for this evening? --I always have my lover. --And how do you love him? --As he would wish.

--Shall we dine together? --If you wish. But what will you give? --This. --Five drachmae? That is for my slave. And me? --Say it yourself. --A hundred.

--Where do you live? --In that blue house. --At what time do you wish me to come seek you? --At once if you should care. --At once. --Lead on.

THE TORN DRESS

Ho! by the two goddesses, who is the brute who put his foot upon my dress? --One who loves you. --He's a block-head. --I was clumsy, pardon me.

The idiot! my yellow dress is all torn up the back, and if I walk the streets like this they'll take me for a wretched girl who serves inverted Venus.

--Won't you stop? --I think he still is speaking to me! --Are you going to leave me when you are so angry? ... you will not answer? Alas! I dare not say another word.

--I surely must go home to change my dress. --And mayn't I come with you? --Who is your father? --He's the rich ship--owner, Nikias. --You have lovely eyes, I pardon you.

JEWELS

A diadem of pierced gold crowns my white and narrow forehead. Five golden chainlets, hung from cheek to cheek, swing from my hair by two large golden hasps.

Upon my arms, which Iris [6] herself would envy, thirteen silver bracelets rise in tiers. How heavy they are! But these are weapons; I know an enemy who has felt their weight.

I am truly clothed in gold. My breasts are cased beneath two golden plates. The statues of the gods are not all as rich as I am.

And I wear about my heavy robe, a girdle worked with silver. You can read these verses on it: "Love me always; but do not be unhappy if I should deceive you thrice a day."

THE IMPARTIAL ONE

As soon as he enters the room, no matter what he be (and can it matter?): "Behold," I say to the slave, "what a handsome man! and how happy a courtesan is."

I call him Adonis, Ares or Herakles, according to his face, or the Old Man of the Seas, if his locks are silver-pale. And then what disdain I show for frivolous youth!

"Ah!" I say, "if tomorrow I had no need to pay my florist or my goldsmith, how I should love to say to you: 'I do not want your gold! I am your slave, impassioned!'"

Then, when he has clasped his arms behind my shoulders, I see a handsome boatman, like an image most divine, passing across the starry sky of my transparent lids.

CLEAR WATER OF THE BASIN

"Clear water of the basin, silent mirror, tell me of my beauty. --Bilitis, or whoever you may be, Tethys [7] or mayhap lovely Amphitrite, you are beautiful, oh, know it well!

"Your face bends over, 'neath your heavy hair, thick with perfumes and entwined flowers. Your tender lids can scarcely open, and your thighs are wearied by the thrusts of love.

"Your body, weighted by your heavy breasts, displays fine nail-marks and the deep blue scars made by ardent kisses. Your arms are reddened by the fast embrace. Each wrinkle in your skin has been beloved."

--"Clear water of the basin, your freshness brings repose. Receive me, who am truly tired. Bear away the tints upon my cheeks, the perspiration of my belly and the memory of the night.

DESIRE

At night, they left us on a high white terrace, fainting among the roses. Warm perspiration flowed like heavy tears from our armpits, running on our breasts. An overwhelming pleasure-lust flushed our thrown-back heads.

Four captive doves, bathed in four different perfumes, fluttered silently above our heads. Drops of scent fell from their wings upon the naked women. I was streaming with the odor of the iris.

Oh, weariness! I laid my cheek upon a young girl's belly, who cooled her body with my humid hair. My open mouth was drunken with her saffron-scented skin. She slowly closed her thighs about my neck.

I dreamed, but an exhausting dream awakened me: the iynx, bird of night-desires, sang madly from afar. I coughed and shivered. An arm, as languid as a flower, rose in the air, stretching towards the moon.

THE INN

Inn-keeper, we are four. Give us a room with two beds. It is too late now to return to the city, and the rain has split the roads.

Bring us a basket of figs, some cheese and black wine; but first take off my sandals and wash my feet, for the mud is tickling me.

You'll have two basins of water brought to the room, a full lamp, a krater [8] and a kylix. You'll shake the covers and beat up all the pillows.

But the beds must be of good solid maple, and the planks silent! Tomorrow you will not awaken us.

DOMESTICITY

Four slaves watch my house: two robust Thracians at the door, a Sicilian in the kitchen, and a docile Phrygian mute at my bed.

The two Thracians are handsome men. They have sticks in their hands with which to chase poor lovers, and a hammer to nail upon the wall the garlands which are sent to me.

The Sicilian is a rare cook; I paid twelve minae for him. No other cook knows how to prepare fried croquettes and poppy-cakes as he does.

The Phrygian bathes me, coifs me, plucks my hair. She sleeps in my room each morning, and three nights of each month she takes my place beside my lovers.

THE BATH

Child, keep watch upon the door, and do not let any passers-by come in, for I and six young girls with lovely arms are going secretly to bathe in the basin's tepid pool.

We only want to laugh and swim a while. Let lovers stay outside. We'll drench our legs in the water, and, seated on the marble edge, play dice.

We'll play ball too. But let no lovers enter; our hair is too wet, our throats have gooseflesh and the ends of our fingers are wrinkled.

Besides, whoever found us naked would regret it! Bilitis is not Athene, but she only shows herself at her own hours and she punishes eyes that are too ardent.

TO HER BREASTS

Flesh in blossom, oh, my breasts! how rich and heavy you are with desire! My breasts in my hands, how soft you are, and with what mellow warmths and young perfumes.

Formerly you were frozen like the breasts of a statue, and hard as senseless marble. Since you have softened I cherish you more, you who have been loved.

Your smooth and swelling form is the pride of my nut-brown body. Whether I bind you in the golden gauze or free you naked to the open air, you precede me with your splendor.

Be happy, then, tonight. If my fingers give forth soft caresses, you alone will know until the dawn: for tonight, Bilitis has paid Bilitis.

MYDZOURIS

Mydzouris, little baggage, cry no more. You are my friend. If the women hurt you again, 'tis I who will answer them. Come to my arms and dry your tears.

Yes, I know you are a dreadful child, and that your mother taught you early to try out all the passions. But you are young, and that is why you can do nothing that will not be charming.

The mouth of a girl of fifteen stays pure in spite of everything. The lips of a hoary woman, although she be a virgin, are defiled; for the only disgrace is to grow old, and we are not stigmatized except by wrinkles.

Mydzouris, I like your frank eyes, your bold and shameless name, your laughing voice, your light-built body. Come home with me and you will be my aide, and when we go out together in the street, the women will say "Hail" to you again.

THE TRIUMPH OF BILITIS

The processionaries carried me in triumph, me, Bilitis, naked in a shell-shaped car, into which all through the night slaves had stripped the petals from ten thousand roses.

I was resting, hands behind my neck, my feet alone were shod in gold, my body softly stretched upon the bed formed by my warm hair mingled with cool petals.

Twelve children with winged shoulders served me as a goddess; some carried a shade and others moistened me with perfumes or burned incense in the rostrum of the car.

And round about I heard the roaring murmur of the crowd, while the breath of its desire was an aura to my nakedness, amidst the blue fog of the aromatics.

TO THE WOODEN GOD

Oh, Venerable Priapos! wooden god that I had fastened in the marble border of my bath, it is not wrongly, guardian of the orchards, that you keep watch here o'er the courtesans.

God, we did not buy you to sacrifice to you our maidenhood. Naught can return that which no longer is, and the zealots of Pallas do not run the streets of Amathus.

No. Formerly you watched over the tresses of the trees, the blooms well-watered, the heavy, tasteful fruits. That is why we have chosen you.

Preserve today our blond heads, the open poppies of our lips and the violets of our eyes. Preserve the solid fruits of our breasts and give us lovers who resemble you. [9]

DANCER WITH CASTANETS

You tie your sounding crotals to your airy hands, Myrrhinidion my dear, and no sooner have you taken off your dress, than you stretch your tensing limbs. How pretty you are with arms flung in the air, arched flanks and rouge-red breasts!

You begin: your feet step one before the other, daintily hesitate, and softly slide. With body waving like a scarf, you caress your trembling skin and desire bathes your long and fainting eyes.

Suddenly you clap your castanets! Arch yourself on tiptoe, shake your flanks, fling your legs, and may your crashing hands call all the lusts in hordes about your fiercely twisting body.

Let us applaud wildly, whether, smiling over your shoulder, you twitch your convulsed and strongly-muscled croup, or undulate, almost stretched abroad, to the rhythm of your ardent memories.

THE FLUTE PLAYER

Melixo, with tight-locked legs and body bent, your arms before you, you slip your light and double flute between your wine-wet lips and play above the couch where Teleas still embraces me.

Am I not unwise, I who hire so young a girl to lighten my laborious hours; am I not unkind, I who thus display her nude to my lovers' prying eyes?

No, Melixo, little musician, you are a stalwart friend. Yesterday you did not hesitate to change your flute when I despaired of accomplishing a trying love-affair. But you are safe.

For well I know what you are thinking of. You wait the end of this excessive night, which exasperates you cruelly and in vain, and at the ghost of dawn you'll run the streets with your only friend Psyllos, to your little hollowed couch.

THE WARM GIRDLE

"You believe you do not love me any more, oh, Teleas! and for a month you've passed your nights at table, as though the fruits and wines and honey could make you forget my mouth. You think you do not love me any more, poor fool!"

And saying that I untied my girdle, still moist with a slight perspiration, and wrapped it round his head. It was still warm with the heat of my belly; the perfume of my skin was wafted from its closely knitted mesh.

He breathed it in long draughts, his eyes tight-closed, then I felt that he was coming back to me and I even saw quite clearly his aroused desires which he did not hide from me; but I was able to resist them, by a ruse.

95

"Ah! no, my friend. Tonight Lysippos has me. Farewell!" And I added, as I fled: "Oh! glutton of fruits and vegetables! Bilitis' little garden has one fig, but it's a good one!"

TO A HAPPY HUSBAND

I envy you, Agorakrites, for having so zealous a wife. 'Tis she herself who tends the stable, and in the morning, instead of making love, she waters the beasts.

And you rejoice in it. How many others, you say, think only of base pleasures, 'wake the night, sleep all day and still ask of adultery a criminal satiety.

Yes, your wife works in the stable. They even say she has a thousand caresses to bestow upon the youngest of your asses. Ah! ha! what a handsome animal! He has a black spot over both his eyes.

They say she plays between his hoofs, beneath his soft grey belly... But they who say these things are slanderers. If your ass pleases her, Agorakrites, it is, without a doubt, because your expression reminds her of its own.

TO ONE WHO HAS STRAYED

The love of women is more beautiful than all the loves we can experience, and even you would think so, Kleon, if your soul were truly amorous; but you only dream of vanities.

You waste your nights in cherishing these youths, who have no true perception of our worth. Just look at them!

How ugly they all are! Compare their round heads to our heavy hair; seek our white breasts upon their hardened chests.

Beside their narrow flanks, take note of our luxuriant haunches, an ample couch, especially hollowed for the lover's use. Say finally what other human lips, if not the ones that they would like to have, can so exalt the pleasures?

You are ill, oh Kleon! but a girl can make you well. Go seek out young Satyra, the daughter of my neighbor Gorgo. Her croup is a rose in the sunlight, and she'll not refuse you the pleasure that she herself prefers.

INTIMACIES

You ask why I am now a Lesbian, oh, Bilitis? But what flute-player is not lesbian a little? I am poor; I have no bed; I sleep with her who wishes me, and thank her with whatever charms I have.

We danced quite naked when we still were small; you know what dances, oh, my dear!: the twelve desires of Aphrodite. We look at one another, compare our nakedness, and find ourselves so pretty.

During the long night we become inflamed for the pleasure of the guests; but our ardour is not feigned, and we feel it so much that sometimes one of us entices her willing friend behind the doors.

How can we then love men, who are rude with us? They seize us like whores, and leave before we can attain our pleasure. You who are a woman, you know what I feel. You pleasure others as *you* would be pleased.

THE COMMAND

"Hear me, old girl. In three days I shall give a festival. I must have a novel entertainment, You will rent me all your girls. How many have you, and say, what can they do?"

"--I have seven. Three dance the kordax with the scarf and phallos. Nephele of the glossy armpits will imitate the love of doves between her rosy breasts.

A singer in a broidered peplos will sing the songs of Rhodes, accompanied by flute-blowers with myrtle-garlands twined about their chestnut limbs."

--That's well. Have them freshly shaven, bathed and perfumed from head to foot, ready for other games should they be asked. Go give my orders. Farewell."

THE MASQUE OF PASIPHAË

[10]

At a debauch given by two young men and some cour-tesans, at my home, where love flowed out like wine, Da-malis, to celebrate her name, danced the Masque of Pasiphaë.

She had had two masks, a cow and a bull, made at Ki-tion, one for herself, and one for Karmantides. She wore two terrible horns, and on her croup a long and hairy tail.

The other women, led by me, and holding flowers and torches, turned to each other's arms with anguished cries, and we caressed Damalis with our trailing hair.

Her sighs, our songs and the dancing of our loins lasted even longer than the night. The empty room is still damp and warm. I look at my reddened knees and the Kios wine-cups with roses swimming in them.

THE JUGGLERESS

When the rays of dawn were mingling with the feeble torches' glow, I had a dissolute, nimble flutist join the orgy; she trembled slightly, being slightly cold.

Praise the little purple-lidded girl, with short hair and impertinent sharp breasts, clothed solely in a girdle hung with jet-black iris-stems and yellow ribbons.

Praise her! for she was clever and performed trying feats of skill. She juggled hoops and did not break a thing, and hopped right through them like a grasshopper.

Sometimes she walked on hands and feet, making a wheel of them. Or better,. legs in air and knees apart, she bent far back and laughing touched the earth.

THE FLOWER DANCE

Anthis, the Lydian dancer, has seven veils about her. She unrolls the yellow veil and her jet-black tresses spread upon the air. The rosy-veil slides from her mouth. The white veil falling shows her naked arms.

She frees her little breasts from the opening scarlet veil. She drops the green one from her round and double croup. She draws the blue veil from her shoulders, but she still retains the last transparent one, pressing it upon her puberty.

The young men plead with her; she shakes her head. Only at the music of the flutes she tears it off a bit, then altogether, and with the gestures of the dance she plucks the fresh young flowers of her body,

Singing: "Where are my roses, where my perfumed violets! Where are my sprays of parsley! --Here are my roses, and I give them to you. There are my violets, do you care for any? There are my lovely curling parsley wisps."

VIOLENCE

No, you shall not take me by force, and do not think you will, oh, Lamprias! If you have heard that Parthenis was raped, know then she met her ravisher half-way, for we cannot be enjoyed without our invitation.

Oh! do your best, make your strongest effort. See, you have fallen short, although I scarce defend myself. I shall not call for help. And I shall not even struggle; but I move. Poor friend, you've fallen short again, I see.

Continue. This little game is funny. More especially since I know that I shall win. One more unhappy pass and perhaps you'll not be so disposed to prove the weakness of your feeble lust.

WILLY POGÁNY

Butcher, what are you doing! Cur, you are breaking my wrists! and this knee, this knee which disembowels me! Ah! now, what a pretty conquest, to rape a young girl on the ground, in tears.

SONG

The first one gave me a necklace, a necklace of pearls worth a city, with temples and palaces, treasures and slaves.

The second wrote poetry for me. He said that my tresses were black as the night's, and my eyes were as blue as the day's.

The third one was handsome; so handsome, that his mother would blush when she kissed him. He put his hands on my knees, and his lips he would press to my feet.

You, you have said nothing to me. You have given me naught, being poor. And you are not overly handsome, but you are the one that I love.

ADVICE TO A LOVER

If you would be beloved of a woman, young friend, no matter what she may be, do not tell her you want her, but see that she sees you each day, and then disappear, to return.

If she speaks to you, you may be amorous, without being eager at all. She will come to you, quite of herself.

Know enough then to take her by force, the day she intends to give way.

When you receive her in bed, neglect your own pleasure. The hands of an amorous woman are trembling and bear no caress. Excuse them from being active.

But for yourself, no repose. Kiss her until you are breathless. Allow her no sleep, though she begs you. Always kiss that part of her body toward which she may turn her eyes.

FRIENDS FOR DINNER

Myromeris and Maskale, my friends, come with me, I have no lover for tonight, and couched on beds of byssos we'll pleasantly discourse through dinner-time.

A night of rest will do you good: you'll sleep in my bed, unpainted and uncoiffed. Put on a simple woolen tunic and leave your jewels in the jewel-box.

No one here will make you dance to admire your legs or the heavy movements of your loins. No one will ask you for the sacred Figures, to judge if you be rightly amorous.

And I have not asked, for our diversion, two auletrides [11] with lovely mouths, but rather two large pots of well-browned peas, some honeyed cakes and fried croquettes and my last skin of Kios wine.

THE TOMB OF A YOUNG COURTESAN

Here lies the fragile body of Lydia, little dove, the happiest of all the courtesans, who, more than any other, cared for orgies, and floating hair, soft dances and hya-cinth-colored tunics.

More than any other she adored the savorous throat-caresses, kisses on the check, games that the lamp alone is witness of, and love which breaks the body with its strength. And now she is a little shade.

But, before she was entombed, her hair was marvelous-ly dressed, and she was laid in roses; the very slab that covers her is soaked with essences and sweet perfumes.

Sacred earth, nurse of all that is, gently receive the poor dead girl, cradle her in your arms, oh, Mother! and all about the headstone of the grave permit no thorns and prickly nettle-growths, but cause white and tender violets to spring.

THE LITTLE FLOWER-VENDOR

"Yesterday," Naïs said to me, "I was in the square, when a little girl in scarlet rags and tatters walked up and of-fered roses to a cluster of young men. And this is what I heard:

'Buy something from me. --Explain yourself, little crea-ture, for we don't know what you're selling: yourself? your roses? or both of them together? --If you buy all the-se flowers, I will give you mine for nothing.

--And how much do you want for all your roses? --My mother must have six oboli, or I'll be beaten like a bitch. --Follow us and you shall have a drachma. --Then should I go and get my little sister?'

And both of them followed these men. They had no breasts, Bilitis. They did not even know how to smile. They trotted off like kids led to the slaughter."

DISPUTE

Ah! by Aphrodite, there you are! offal! filth! stink! trash! slut! clumsy! good-for-nothing! dirty sow! Don't try to flee me, but come here; come closer!

Let me see this sailor's wench who does not even know how to fold her robe over her shoulder, and who paints so badly that her eyebrow's black runs down her cheeks in streams of ink!

You are Phoenician; go lie with your own race. While as for me, my father was Hellenic; I've rights o'er all who wear the petasos. [12] And all the others, if it pleases me.

Don't stop again in my street, or I'll send you to Hades to make love to Charon, and I'll say, quite justly, too: "May the earth rest lightly on you!", so that the dogs can dig you up again.

MELANCHOLY

I shiver, the night is chill and the woods are wet. Why have you brought me here? isn't my big bed softer than all this pebble-studded moss?

My flowery robe will get all grass-stained and my hair all tangled up with little twigs; my elbow, look at my elbow, how dirty it is already with wet earth.

One time, however, I used to follow *him* into the wood... Ah! leave me awhile. I am sad this evening. Don't speak, just leave me, hands upon my eyes.

Really, can't you wait! are we brute beasts for you to take us so I Leave me alone. You shall not open my lips nor yet my knees. For fear of crying, my very eyes are closed.

LITTLE PHANION

Stranger, stop, look who is signalling you: 'tis little Phanion of Kôs, she is well worth your choice.

See, her hair is curled like parsley, her skin is soft as the down of a woodland bird. She is small and brown. And she converses well.

If you should follow her, she would not ask you all your voyage-money; no, just a drachma or a pair of sandals.

You'll find she has a good bed in her house, fresh figs and milk and wine, and if it should be cold there'll be a fire.

INFORMATION

If you should like, oh! halting passer-by, slim thighs and high-strung flanks, a hard, strong throat and knees which clasp, go seek out Plango, she who is my friend.

If you are looking for a laughing girl with round luxurious breasts, a fragile build, plump buttocks and lovely hollowed flanks, go to the corner of this street where Spidhorodellis has her domicile.

But if long tranquil hours in a courtesan's arms, her soft skin, the belly's warmth and odor of her tresses pleases you, go look for Milto, you will be satisfied.

But do not expect much love; profit by her experience. One can ask everything of a woman, when she is nude, when it is night and a hundred drachmae lie upon the hearth.

THE VENDOR OF WOMEN

Who is there? --I am the woman-vendor. Open your door, Sostrata, I'll give you two good reasons. This one first. Approach, Anasyrtolis, and undress yourself. --She is a little heavy.

--She's a beauty. Besides, she does the kordax; and knows eighty songs. --Turn around. Raise your arms. Show your hair. Put up your foot. Now smile. That's good.

--This one now. --She is too young! --Oh! not at all! She was twelve the day before yesterday, and you cannot teach her a thing. --Take off your tunic. Let's see? No, she is thin.

--I only ask a mina for her. --And the first? --Two minae thirty. --Three minae for the both? --Done. --Come in and wash yourselves. And you, farewell.

STRANGER

Stranger, go no further in the town. You'll not find younger or more expert girls at any other place besides my own. I am Sostrata, known beyond the sea.

See this one whose eyes are green as water on the grass. You do not wish her? Here are other eyes, black as the violet and hair three cubits long.

I have some better still. Xantho, open your cyclas. Stranger, her breasts are firm as quinces, touch them. And her lovely belly, you can see, bears the three Kyprian folds.

I bought her with her sister, who is not yet quite old enough for love, but who is her useful helper. By the two goddesses! you are of noble blood. Phyllis and Xantho, follow the gentleman!

MEMORY OF MNASIDIKA

They danced before each other in swift and fleeting movement; they always seemed to wish to touch each other, but never touched, unless it be their lips.

When they turned their backs in the mazes of the dance, and looked at one another, head on shoulder, the perspiration glistened 'neath their high-uplifted arms, and their fine-spun tresses swished before their breasts.

The languor of their eyes, the fire in their cheeks and the serious expression of their faces, seemed three ardent songs all sung at once. They brushed against each other furtively, they bent their swaying bodies at the hip.

And suddenly they fell, to consummate their tender dance upon the earth... Memory of Mnasidika, it was then that you appeared to me, and everything except your dear sweet image was annoying.

YOUNG MOTHER

Do not think, Myromeris, that because you were a mother your beauty has diminished in the least. Now your body, underneath its robe, has drowned its fragile lines beneath voluptuary softness.

Your breasts are two vast flowers overturned upon your chest, whose cut stems furnish forth a milky sap. Your softer belly melts beneath the hand.

And give a thought now to the little child, born of the ecstasy that once you felt, one evening in the arms of a passer-by whose very name you now no longer know. Dream of her far-away fate.

These eyes, which scarcely open now, one day will be far lengthened by a line of black, and will sow joy or anguish among men by a single flutter of their curling lashes.

THE UNKNOWN

He sleeps. I do not know him. He horrifies me. However, his purse is full of gold, and he gave the slave four drachmae when he entered. I expect a mina for myself.

But I told the Phrygian to go to bed in my place. He was drunk and took her for me. I had rather die in torment than stretch myself alongside of this man.

Alas! I dream of the fields of Tauros... I was a little virgin... Then my breasts were light, and I was so mad with amorous envy that I loathed my married sisters.

What would I not have done to have obtained that which I have refused tonight! Today my breasts are drooping, and in my worn-out heart Eros falls asleep from weariness.

TRICKERY

I awaken. Then he is gone! He left something! No: two empty amphora and some sullied flowers. The rug is red with wine.

I slept, but I am still intoxicated... With whom did I come home? ... Anyhow, we went to bed together. The bed itself is even soaked in sweat.

There might even have been several; the bed is so upset. I can't remember... But someone must have seen them! There is my Phrygian. She still is sleeping, crosswise to the door.

I kick her in the breast and cry: "Bitch, you could not have..." I am so hoarse I cannot speak at all.

THE LAST LOVER

Child, do not go on without having loved me. I still am fair, beneath the cloak of night; you shall see how much warmer my autumn is than any other's spring...

Do not seek the love of virgins. Love is a difficult art in which young girls are not highly versed. I have spent my life in learning it, to give it to my last lover.

You, I know, will be my last lover. Here is my mouth, for which a nation has grown ashen with desire. Here is my hair that the great Psappha sang in measured verse.

I shall gather together for you all that is left of my lost youth. I'll even burn my memories themselves. I'll give you Lykas' flute ... Mnasidika's girdle.

THE DOVE

I have long been lovely; the day is coming when I shall no longer be a woman. Then I'll know rending memories, burning solitary envies, and my tears will bathe my hands.

If life is a long dream, what use is there in resisting it? Now, four and five times every night I ask for amorous joy, and when my flanks are tired I fall asleep where'er my body lies.

At morning I raise my lids and I shiver in my hair. A dove is at my window; I ask it what month it may chance to be. It says: "This is the month in which women are in love."

Ah, whatever month it be, the dove speaks truly, Kypris! And I throw my arms about my lover's neck, and trembling stretch my still torpid legs to the very foot of the tumbled bed.

MORNING RAIN

The night is fading. The stars are far away. Now the very latest courtesans have all gone homewards with their paramours. And I, in the morning rain, write these verses in the sand.

The leaves are loaded down with shining water. The little streams that run across the roads carry earth and trains of dead leaves. The rain, drop by drop, makes holes in my song.

Ah, how sad and lonely I am here! The youngest do not look at me at all; the oldest all have quite forgotten me. 'Tis well. They will learn my verses, and the children of their children...

Here is something neither Myrtale, nor Thaïs, nor Glykera will say, the day their lovely cheeks grow sagged with age. Those who will love when I am gone, will sing my songs together, in the dark.

TRUE DEATH

Aphrodite! inexorable Goddess, thou hast desired that happy youth with lovely curls should fade from me, too, in a few short days. Why did I not die altogether then?

I looked at myself in my mirror: I can no longer smile or even cry. Oh! lovely face that Mnasidika loved, I can't believe that you were really mine.

Can it be that all is ended now! I have not yet lived five times eight short years; I feel that I was born but yesterday, and now it must already be proclaimed: No one will ever love me any more.

I have shorn all my hair, and twined it in my girdle and I offer it to thee, eternal Kypris! I shall not cease from loving thee. This is the last verse of the pious Bilitis.

[1] The Greek quotation as translated by Paton in the Palatine Anthology (XI-34), reads: "Bind my head with narcissus, and let me taste the crooked flute. Anoint my limbs with saffron ointment, wet my gullet with wine of Mytilene, and mate me with a virgin who will love her nest."

[2] *Philommeïdes*: laughter-loving.

[3] *The Mysteries*: Since there is so little known about the Eleusinian mysteries--in fact, there is nothing here to indicate that these were the Mysteries of Eleusis, to which both men and women were admitted (perhaps in separate groups)--it is obvious that M. Louÿs had a rather wide latitude within which to make use of his romantic vein. Needless to say, no initiate would ever have committed the inestimable indiscretion of mentioning the slightest portion of the rite. *Berbeia*: There seems to be no definite information as to who Berbeia may have been, Louÿs having found the name in Athenæus, and carelessly employed it as he chose. Athenæus, quoting from an earlier poet, says it might possibly be the name of some deity or other (3-84-C).

[4] *Pasiphaë*: see below. *Syrinx*: another of the ever-lovely nymphs, who, when pursued by Pan, was sympathetically turned (by the water-nymphs) into a tuft of reeds, thereby furnishing the rustic deity with another deathless instrument. This is the story which should have kept Argus awake, but, when related by Mercury, had uncomfortable results, both for Argus and another of Zeus's mistresses (Io). *Byblis*: daughter of Miletus, who incestuously pursued her brother until discouraged, when she was turned into a fountain.

[5] James Huneker's "*Eighth Deadly Sin. Perfume*" was so flourishing an art in the ancient world, that it merits more than the passing

lamentation which my space permits. Its modern votaries are so dreadfully deficient in olfactory sense that those who are attributed with occult powers in its use, that is to say, women, are most strangely ignorant of its fundamental edicts. In fact, the great decadence into which the use of scents has sadly slipped is responsible for its very occasional use as a substitute rather than as an adjunct to cleanliness. (In deference to the modern world, I may be permitted to qualify this last statement by a wholesome doubt as to whether this usage is wholly restricted to the small horizon of the present). Discovered most likely by accident, its first use was probably as incense, a pleasure-offering to an anthropomorphic god. You could only hope, naïvely, that the god approved your taste. This usage finally became incidental, however, and ancient literature is redolent with passages relating the universal delight in which the scents were held. The *Paradise of the Houris* was paved with musk. *Solomon's Beloved* was a bundle of myrrh and frankincense. The *Cæsars* spent fortunes on perfumes while the populace was starving. *Petronius* has hinted at this fine abuse in his caricature of *Trimalchio*. *Suetonius* has been more explicit in his *Nero*. Athens was flooded with strange oriental scents and sins. The love books of the east will tell you just what tincture should be used to interest, capture, vanquish and seduce. *Ovid* will instruct the Roman maid. All good Athenians floated in billows of perfume. Cosmetic was no minor art itself. Marjoram, apple, ivy, mint and saffron; spikenard and frankincense and myrrh, all vied with the paint-pot and the tinting-brush. If corruption was not cured, then it was covered. (Thus they explain the origin of beauty patches!). *Apollonius* hints that the power of *Circe* was no paltry necromancy; she used a different perfume for each portion of her body (*ô douceur, ô poison!*). Small wonder that her victims were real, or even merely sad symbolic swine! *Odysseus* only knew the anti-aphrodisiac. No matter. All the great magicians and enchantresses knew and understood the science of the nose. That the ability to concoct and blend, apply and harmonize these precious essences has perished almost wholly from the earth can be no better typified than in the woman who buys and uses a scent because she "likes it," with no regard as to its fitness for her. I feel that there is reason for regret.

[6] *Iris*: the female Mercury, Goddess of the Rainbow, which was her steed, and who was furnished appropriately with vari-colored wings.

[7] *Tethys*.--the wife of Oceanus, and mother of the river-gods and Oceanides. *Amphitrite*: the wife of Neptune, who succeeded with her husband to the dominion of the waters in the place of *Tethys* and *Oceanus*, when the Titans were overthrown by *Zeus*, *Poseidon* (Neptune) and *Dis* (Pluto).

[8] *krater* and *kylix*.--otherwise a crater and a calix: wine-vessels.

[9] *lovers who resemble you*: As is so often the case in the *Chansons*, Louÿs has amused himself by attaching a typically Gallic innuendo. The statues of *Priapus* were little more than a stone or wooden shaft surmounted by the god's head, and embellished in front by a formidable phallus.

[10] *Pasiphaë*--whose husband Minos was punished properly through her passion for a bull he chose rather to keep than sacrifice to Poseidon. Representations of this sort must have been very common. Suetonius (*The Twelve Cæsars, Nero XII*) mentions that Nero also illustrated this myth in an amphitheatre constructed in the region of the *Campus Martius*, through the medium of a hollow wooden cow.

[11] *auletrides*: flute-blowers, who combined their musical entertainment with "*d'autres jeux si on les leur demande.*"

[12] *petasos*: "a flat felt hat, with a broad round rim ... said to have been introduced into Greece ... as a distinguishing mark of the *ephebi* (youths)." (*Harper's Dictionary*, supra).

The Tomb of Bilitis

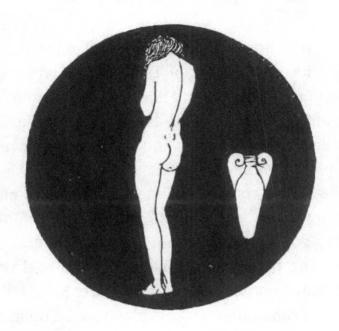

FIRST EPITAPH

In the land where the rivers are born from the sea, and the beds of the streams made of fine flakes of quartz, I, Bilitis, was born.

My mother was Phoenician, my father Damophylos, Hellenic. My mother taught me the sad songs of Byblos, sad as the coming of dawn.

I adored Astarte at Kypros. I knew Psappha at Lesbos. I have sung of how I have loved. If I have lived well, Passerby, tell your daughter.

And do not sacrifice the black goat in my memory; but, as a sweet libation, squeeze her soft dug o'er my tomb.

SECOND EPITAPH

On the dark shores of the Melas, at Tamassos in Pamphylia, I, Bilitis, daughter of Damophylos, first saw the light. I rest far away from my birth-place, you see.

As a child I was taught the loves of Adon and Astarte, the mysteries of holy Syria, and death and the return to She-of-the-full-rounded-eyelids.

If I have been a courtesan, wherein lies the blame? Was this not my work as a woman? Stranger, the Mother-of-Everything guides us. She cannot be wisely ignored.

In gratitude to you who have paused here, I wish you this fate: May you be loved, but not love. Farewell, and in your old age remember that once you gazed on my tomb.

LAST EPITAPH

Beneath the black leaves of the laurel, 'neath the amorous blooms of the rose, 'tis here I am resting forever; I who could weave verses together, I who could make kisses to bloom.

I grew up in the land of the Nymphs; I lived on the island of lovers; I died on the island of Kypris. That is why my name is distinguished, and my monument polished with oil.

Do not weep for me, you who have paused here: my funeral arrangements were sweet; the mourners scratched their cheeks; my mirrors and necklaces rest in my tomb.

And now, on the pale prairies of asphodel, an impalpable shadow, I walk, and the memories of my earthly existence are the joys of my underworld life.

Bibliography

[1]

I--*Bilitis' sæmmtliche Lieder zum ersten Male herausgegeben und mit einem Woerterbuche versehen, von G. Heim.*--Leipzig, 1894.

II--*Les Chansons de Bilitis, traduites du grec pour la premiere fois par P. L.*--Paris, 1895.

III--*Six Chansons de Bilitis, traduites en vers par Mme. Jean Bertheroy.*--Revue pour les jeunes filles, Paris, *Armand Colin, 1896.*

IV--*Twenty-six Songs of Bilitis, translated into German by Richard Dehmel.*--Die Gesellschaft, *Leipzig, 1896.*

V--*Twenty Songs of Bilitis, translated into German by Dr. Paul Goldmann.*--Frankfurter Zeitung, *1896.*

VI--*The Songs of Bilitis, by Pr. von Willamovitz-Moellendorf.*--Goettingsche Gelehrte, *Goettingen, 1896.*

VII--*Eight Songs of Bilitis, translated into Czech by Alexander Backovsky.*--Prague, 1897.

VIII--*Four Songs of Bilitis, translated into Swedish by Gustav Uddgren.*--Nordisk Revy, *Stockholm, 1897.*

IX--*Three Songs of Bilitis, set to music by Claude Debussy.*--Paris, Fromont, 1898.

[1] BIBLIOGRAPHY: Added by Louÿs as further "evidence" for the authenticity of the Bilitis legend. The songs which Claude Debussy set to bewitching music are "*La Chevelure,*" "*La Flûte de Pan*" (*La Flûte*), and "*Le Tombeau des Naïades.*"

Note

Since previous editions of the *Songs of Bilitis* have been complacently unconcerned with the desirability of sympathetic treatment, accurate translation or rhythmic presentation, I offer this version of an extremely lovely book, in all humility, as leaven to their dough, although acutely conscious that the whole is bread, where cake is (this time) sadly in demand.

A. C. B.

Title: *"Translated from the Greek"*:

It was M. Louÿs' little *mot* to ascribe these "songs" to a courtesan who, he declares, was a contemporary of Sappho. To heighten this false appearance of translation he has written his clever "Life" of Bilitis, as well as included several songs in the table of contents which he labels "not translated." There is, however, a strangely haunting ring, muffled, though not too carefully disguised ... a curiously Gallic undertone, which echoes incongruous down the centuries from Bilitis to us, and makes her the great creation that she is. M. Louÿs took Voltaire's sage advice. Since he has thus committed himself, the following brief notes will be concerned only with the elucidation of the ancient words employed, and occasional references to legends and institutions which may be unfamiliar to the present reader. A mock-philological study of the sources from which Louÿs drew material for this book would be amusing, but would have little sound scholastic value. He will be found to have dipped delicately into such writers of the *Palatine Anthology* as *Philodemus, Hedylus, Meleager, Denys, Paulus Silentiarius* and *Asclepiades*. In most cases he has been content merely to elaborate a phrase or idea; in a very few others he has charmingly appropriated a complete epigram, changing it but slightly to suit his occult purposes. Sappho herself has been "pilfered" for the chanson he calls "Love"! Louÿs' culpability in this respect is distinctly limited, however, for by far the greatest part of the *Chansons de Bilitis* is his original creation, and must accordingly be judged as such.

www.ingramcontent.com/pod-product-compliance
Lightning Source LLC
LaVergne TN
LVHW051806180125
801629LV00003B/686